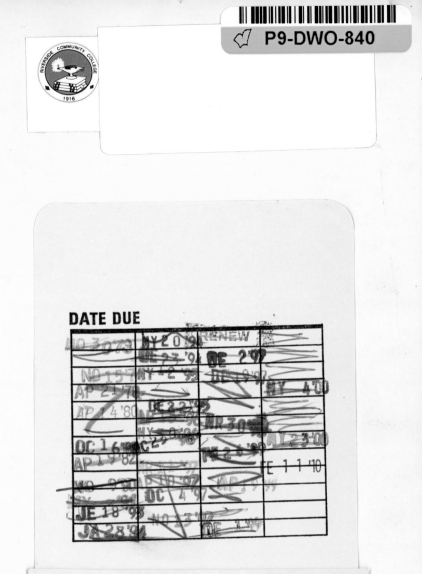

Brahms : A Critical Study

Brahms
A Critical Study

by Burnett James

Praeger Publishers
New York · Washington

Books That Matter

Published in the United States of America in 1972
by Praeger Publishers, Inc., 111 Fourth Avenue,
New York, N.Y. 10003
© Burnett James, 1972

Library of Congress Catalog Card Number: 78-165884

Printed in Great Britain

Preface

Brahms literature in German was once generous and regular, but it has trailed off for many years now. Brahms literature in English was also fairly copious once, when Brahms's temperament and music made a strong appeal to the English and to English musicians; but it too has trailed off and is now pretty thin on the ground. Yet, from the strictly biographical or the directly analytical viewpoints, both are probably adequate when in print. The larger part of Brahms's life was not eventful: after the regrettable experiences in his Hamburg boyhood and the shocking impact of the Schumann tragedy, his life pursued a fairly even course, largely because he himself determined that it should. Thus there are few dramatic high lights, virtually no 'incidents' to be blown up to make a pressman's holiday, and almost certainly no lurid scandals yet to be revealed. Max Kalbeck probably set down all that is really important; later writers have filled in the gaps, filled out the details. Analytically, Brahms was long ago uniquely served by Edwin Evans, Senior, in the great four-volume *Handbook* covering every one of Brahms's compositions. We may disagree with Evans in part, but with the *Handbook* before us the mechanics of Brahms's music is comprehensively revealed and there is no call to go over it all again. Commentaries by Tovey and others expand and enlarge upon the central matter.

Thus my own book is neither straight biography of everyday fact nor pedagogic analysis of this, that and the other among Brahms's compositions. Since I am persuaded that both these tasks have been adequately carried out (add, of course, Florence May to the biographical tally, perhaps for the English or English-speaking reader, best of all), I am not going to make a big issue of either. Inevitably, since a composer is (was) a man, he lived a life and that life must be noticed; and being a composer he wrote music and that too must be looked at with eyes of some analytical intent. But over and beyond that, or those, every artist, if he is to have meaning for a later age, must receive revaluation in that age and in the light of its specific beliefs, lack of beliefs, ideas, even fashionable attitudes, even if those have to be merely knocked on the head as irrelevant because trivial. Ideas and beliefs matter; attitudes are the waste product of the age.

There are two ways of writing about a man, just as there are fundamentally two types of criticism—the academic and the existential. I make no bones that this book is intended as an existential biography of Johannes Brahms. It offers no gesture towards the academic variety, not because I have a poor view of that form and species of literature but simply because, as I have said, it has been done and well done and need not be done over. But the existential approach can never be 'done' because it is interpretation of fact rather than presentation and analysis of fact, although fact must still be at the bottom of it. Of course there are the elements of both in both: it is essentially a question of bias and emphasis. Either way, this is neither a handbook to Brahms's works nor a documentary upon his life. It is, quite simply, an attempt to see and understand Johannes Brahms from the central viewpoint of the second half of the twentieth century, for I think that is all that is worth doing and all that can be done. If having done it I feel closer to Brahms than ever before, that is largely because the task has entailed continual intimacy with Brahms's music over many months—not to find out if it is good or bad (hardly a question worth asking, except maybe as a slightly desperate counter of impotence) but more directly, if more enigmatically, to try to find out what is with Brahms from the bridge of the 1970s; from, that is, today's particular perspective.

B. J.

Checkendon, 1971.

Contents

List of Illustrations

Acknowledgments

The author and publishers wish to acknowledge with gratitude permission to quote from copyright material as follows:

To George Allen & Unwin Ltd, London, and Simon & Schuster, Inc., New York, for *A History of Western Philosophy* by Bertrand Russell; John Farquharson Ltd, for *The Musical World of Robert Schumann* by Henry Pleasants (published by Victor Gollancz Ltd); Macmillan & Co. Ltd, for *Letters to and from Joseph Joachim*, translated by Nora Bickley; William Reeves Booksellers Ltd, for the *Life of Johannes Brahms* by Florence May; George Weidenfeld & Nicolson Ltd, London, and Alfred A. Knopf, Inc., New York, for *Johannes Brahms: His Work and Personality* by Hans Gal; and Edward Arnold Ltd, for *Letters of Clara Schumann and Johannes Brahms, 1853-96*, edited by Dr Berthold Litzmann.

The author and publishers also extend their gratitude to Mrs Heidkamp of Deutsche Grammophon Gesellschaft, Hamburg, and to Mr Ray Crick of the Decca Record Co., London, for providing photographs.

1 The Roots and the Soil

Brahms

Brahms liked to say that the two most important events of his lifetime were the completion of the Bachgesellschaft Edition and the
foundation of the German Empire by Bismarck. He spoke wisely
and true. These were the twin poles of his life: his musical inheritance upon the one hand, his national inheritance upon the other.
From these two all else stems.

In the history of German music Johannes Brahms was the linear
descendant of Beethoven but the true heir of Bach. He came out of
Protestant North Germany, from the proud Hanseatic free city of
Hamburg, and he came into the potent nineteenth century which
was to change the entire course of human history and revolutionize
the destiny of man. It often appears that history 'places' great men,
and creative artists perhaps more than any, in exactly the right
context; or, as it is differently put, that 'the hour produces the
man'. Yet there is an over-simplification here; an assumption
based upon appearance rather than reality. What is nearer to truth
and more penetrating is that the creative spirit in the individual

responds to the physical and non-physical environments in which at any one time it chances to find itself.

And there is more chance about it than we usually suspect. Certainly the process seems, and unmistakably is, reciprocal. The 'child of the times' is true to some extent, and must be true, for none can live and work in a vacuum; but also it is true that, as one might choose to form it, the times are of the child: the child in this sense, in the meaning of the major creative force and spirit, is as much maker of the age as product of it. It operates all through, can be detailed and proposed in every era, upon every plane; it is true of Shakespeare, Dante, Goethe, Yeats, Eliot; is true of Bach, Mozart, Beethoven, Wagner, Mahler, Schoenberg; is true as far and as complex as you have to see and understand it. And it is quite surely true of Brahms, who had great love and reverence for the past, a firm sense of the present and the spirit of prophecy for the future in the deepest, most meaningful, sense, not as the self-consciously 'forward-looking' 'progressives' have, but upon that ground where all truly creative, unquestionably responsive, artists in whatever medium are and can never help being.

Despite the allegiance to Beethoven and the involvement with Schumann, Bach was the key figure in Brahms's musical life and potency: Bach who rose from a shattered Germany and the ashes of the Thirty Years War and of whom Wagner said, with typical exaggeration but true insight, that he was 'the history of the inner life of the German mind during that awful century when the German people was utterly extinguished'. Bach, in fact, or rather the rediscovery of Bach, was a major force in the evolution of German music in the nineteenth century, the century of German reunification and rise to world power and influence. He was revered by Schumann, by Wagner, by Brahms, also by Chopin, and his informing spirit had touched significantly the final years of Mozart's short life before the dawning of the new century and the Romantic era.

For Germany and German music, Bach was not only incomparable universal genius but even more symbol of the life and the resurrection. During and after the Thirty Years War, when Germany as a nation was destroyed and a new age of savage barbarism inaugurated, the religious force remained and held its strength. And Bach was essentially a pinnacle of religious man. No one can understand the resurgent Germany of the nineteenth century, with its literature and its music, can penetrate the heart of German Romanticism, also in its literature and its music, without referring back to and comprehensively understanding Bach and that older Germany out of which he arose and whose complete expression he became.

The nineteenth century was not of the 'religious age', and Brahms was not in the older and traditional sense a specimen of religious man. He had his religion all right, as well as his deep attraction to the Bible. But it was or may be called a 'humanist religion', sceptical agnosticism leading ultimately to stoic resignation; certainly in keeping with the currents of thought and feeling, the pressures of change and evolving science of the times; certainly not ignoble. In an age of doubt man's accepted place in the universe was inevitably challenged: some, like Wagner, thrust outwards and onwards, taking up, if in part unconsciously, the evolutionary cudgels; others like Brahms turned inwards to the fount and seed-bed of national and racial inheritance, and thus carried the process forward by other means.

Brahms was by nature and temperament both socially and musically conservative; but not in the negative, restrictive sense of wilful reaction and resistance to progress, rather that deep-dyed conservatism which is also in its way the servant of progress but from the reverse side, both being essential to the forward thrust of the whole. It was this two-way split and thrust which lay at the root of the Brahms-Wagner controversy, which disfigured the musical life of the mid nineteenth century, and which must have in its place a full chapter to itself.

The bed of Brahms's musical semen was German folk-song. What Lutheran chorale was to Bach, folk-song was to Brahms. No need to hark back to Brahms's own reported words that whenever he was stuck for a melody he thought of a German folk-tune: that is too bland and too obvious; Brahms once again taking the solemn ones for a joyride probably. Yet all through his music is the artistic flowering of German folk-melody, growing out of the rich German

3

historical soil, often so subtly mixed art- and folk-theme that it becomes impossible to tell less where one begins and the other ends than the true balance and interaction of the two in the final blend.

The typical Brahmsian *melos*, so far as it is precisely identifiable, is a complex mingling of natural and contrived elements. (I do not use the word 'contrived' in any pejorative sense, but simply as invented or devised, much as many of Beethoven's themes, upon the evidence of his sketch-books, were 'contrived' out of frequently crude initial ideas, and as indeed may be said of most art-themes. Those who despise Brahms and hold that nearly all his music was contrived in the other and deprecatory meaning will rejoice in the appearance of the term so early on in a book; but those who understand and have no axe to grind will see the true relevance.) Brahms's indebtedness to German folk-song was the direct result of his German temperament, the inherent saturation of his mind and spirit in the totality of Germanism, both in the times in which he lived and in the long historical perspectives of the individual and collective unconscious.

Yet it was conscious also, and perhaps first of all. Because of the dislocation of German history in the seventeenth century with the wreckage and destruction of the old German dream in the aftermath of the Treaty of Westphalia in 1648, which brought about the fragmentation of Germany and the complete loss of national identity, followed by nearly a hundred years of chaos with many small princedoms struggling to rebuild their economies on a purely local basis, pride in race and nation for the Germans in the nineteenth century when reunification became reality was different from what it was for most other peoples. The 'awful century' of which Wagner spoke had made it inevitable that the resurgence of the German nation and the German national spirit would come in with particular force and passion.

Throughout the eighteenth century a series of military campaigns was fought on German soil, and although in them German troops fought alongside the British, most had nothing to do with the interests or concerns of the German peoples. Issues at stake were the Spanish succession and the rivalry between France and

England in India and the New World—William Pitt declared that the British conquest of Canada would be effected on the plains of Germany. The one issue which did directly concern Germany was the rivalry between Prussia and Austria in the names of Frederick the Great and the Empress Maria Theresa. After the Treaty of Westphalia had broken up the old Germany, it soon became obvious that the only developing units large and powerful enough to undertake the historical process of German reunification and centralization were what became known as Prussia and Austria, both in this context amalgamations of two or more territorial institutions. Both Prussia and Austria had grown up to combat threats to Europe from the 'heathen' east—Prussia fought the Russians and the Slavs, Austria opposed the westward intrusions of the Turks.

But the growing power of Prussia at length became a danger to her neighbours, confirmed by the accession of Frederick the Great and his immediate seizure of the Austrian province of Silesia, in contravention of a promise given by his father, Frederick William I, at what was known as the Pragmatic Sanction, which provided that the Hapsburg Emperor Charles VI should be succeeded by his daughter Maria Theresa.

This act of aggression sparked off the Seven Years War, in 1756, in which Austria, France, Sweden and Russia combined to crush the upstart ruler. Britain and Hanover supported Frederick, but the combined weight against him would have been too great and would probably have turned the Prussian defeat at Kunersdorf into the overthrow of the Prussian State had it not been for the sudden death of the Empress Elizabeth of Russia, Frederick's sworn enemy, and the succession of her nephew Peter III, who was his firm admirer. This brought peace followed by the First Partition of Poland, when Frederick and Peter divided the spoils of the old kingdom of Poland which had fallen into chaos and confusion between the warring parties. Maria Theresa was persuaded into agreeing to this piece of business, but to the end of her life she regretted it and thought it a stain upon the honour of her reign and her House. Prussia under Frederick the Great had thus manœuvred herself into a position of direct rivalry with Austria for the leadership in the German principalities, although the

5

elimination of Poland meant that that there was no 'buffer' between Germany and Russia, and would not be again until 1919. Since the armies of the Empress Elizabeth had penetrated deep into Germany and threatened Berlin, this was to have profound consequences for Europe throughout the nineteenth century and into the twentieth.

But the next threat came from the west. At the turn of the century Napoleon's victorious armies of the French Revolution marched into Germany and routed the cluster of small principalities, moribund bishoprics and scattered Free Cities. Napoleon was on the way to becoming master of Europe, and he was not particular about how he did it. Those who at first saw in the doctrine of Liberty, Equality and Fraternity a potent force of change and progress, soon became aware of the other side of the coin, and what had at first appeared as a movement of liberation was revealed as an instrument of new tyranny. The old rivalry between Prussia and Austria at first worked to Napoleon's advantage, and Prussia pulled out of the fight, leaving Napoleon free to deal with Austria. But Napoleon was busy in North Germany too, and when Hamburg was made into a Department of France, the King of Prussia saw the danger and declared war. It made no difference and the Prussians were decisively defeated at Jena and Auerstädt. Thus Napoleon now controlled virtually the whole of Germany and directed the policies of both Prussia and Austria.

The French occupation of Germany had a number of long-term effects, of which the most important was the slow build-up of German resistance and the resurgence of the nationalist spirit. And the centre of this resistance was Prussia, where memories of brief glory under Frederick the Great rumbled beneath the surface and refused to be extinguished by intruding Frenchmen. And it became in the end Prussia rather than Austria which led the German resistance to the French, especially after Napoleon's strength had been worn down by the Russian disaster. Prussians under Marshal Blücher fought beside the British at Waterloo; and it was Blücher who was senior German general at the Congress of Vienna held to establish a permanent European peace after the downfall of Napoleon in 1815. Again, the predominance of Prussia in the German resistance to the French was to have far-reaching effects.

Napoleon's occupation of Germany had at least one significant result: the old hotchpotch of small and largely ineffectual autonomous states and principalities was broken down and rationalized. And because of the part Prussia had played in the liberation movement, she gained territory as well as influence; and among the territories accruing to Prussia were the industrial areas of the Ruhr with their huge coalfields. The invention of the steam engine was about to revolutionize transport through its application to rail and water—and this in itself was to play a dominant role in the coming hundred years.

Economic developments and needs were to dictate the future constitution of Europe, as had military ones previously. The growth of the major industries brought about both big movements in population and big increases in the size of the average family. This for the first time made Germany initially as large, population wise, as France, and then larger—in fact the largest numerical force in Europe. The balance of power in Europe was thus significantly altered.

Emotional as well as economic forces were now moving inevitably in the direction of German unification. Many were the new or revived dreams of one German nation, of a real and prospering Deutschland, all symbolized in Heinrich Hoffman von Fallersleben's poem (1841) *Das Lied der Deutschen* sung to Haydn's fine tune from the string quartet, Op. 76, No. 3, nicknamed the 'Emperor' because that same tune, itself known as the 'Emperor's Hymn', had become Austria's national anthem. Von Fallersleben's poem of course has the famous first line 'Deutschland über alles' and thus became a kind of rallying cry for those who looked with passionate conviction to a new and resurgent German nation and concentrated all effort of mind and will to that end, whether it should come eventually as the 'Great Germany' ('Grossdeutschland') which would include Austria, or the 'Little Germany' ('Kleindeutschland') from which Austria would be excluded, the former implying Austrian leadership, the latter making certain of Prussian leadership.

7

A unified Germany, upon whatever basis, had by now become a political and economic necessity, as well as an emotional and spiritual, and thus a popular, one, for democratic ideals from the French Revolution first, and then from the Paris uprisings against reaction of 1830 and 1848, had taken hardly less strong root in Germany.

The first attempts at German unification, made at a gathering of Germanic leaders (including Austrian) at Frankfurt-am-Main in May 1848, failed. As usual, in spite of the dreams and ideals, the delegates could not agree and the conference broke up with nothing solved.

But at the Frankfurt conference was one man who saw clearly into the future and determined to act upon what he saw with unflinching realism—his name, Otto von Bismarck. Bismarck turned away from the 'Great Germany' idea to that of 'Kleindeutschland', excluding Austria. Two factors led Bismarck to that decision, to the founding of a strong, unified German State led by Prussia—the growing industrial power of the Ruhr, which lay within Prussian boundaries, and the historical structure of the Austrian Empire with its large non-German territories. Bismarck saw that if the new Germany was to include Austria, these non-German parts of the Hapsburg Empire must inevitably break away and come under the Russian sphere of influence and would then constitute an unacceptable threat to German security. Thus the Austrian Empire had to be preserved; and with that decision the form of the new Germany was fixed and settled.

It would still take Bismarck nearly a decade of patient manœuvring and strategic diplomacy, plus several wars of limited objective, after he became Prussian Prime Minister in 1862, before he achieved what he set out to achieve; but at the victorious conclusion of the Franco-Prussian War it was done. When the combined leaders of the German states met in the Palace of Versailles in Paris in January 1871 there was little left to do but set the seal upon German unification. This was the culmination of the years of Bismarck's policy of political realism, and King William of Prussia was acclaimed Emperor of Germany. Although there were serious flaws in the solution, and several of the other German leaders thought they had been pushed into something they did not entirely like, the political and economic facts could not be ignored. This was the moment of Bismark's triumph and the vindication, for Germany, of his former policies.

For twenty years Bismarck followed a firm course of political realism, conciliating Germany's neighbours where possible, strengthening her internal and external situation in the light of growing industrial and technological power, and generally keeping European affairs under control. Support for Austria to ensure stability in eastern Europe, conciliation of France (in which he was partly thwarted when his opposition to the total annexation of Alsace and Lorraine was overruled), friendship with England and a cautious eye on Russia and Russian expansionist ambitions: these were the cornerstones of Bismarck's foreign policy. And for the most part it worked. Not everybody liked Bismarck or Bismarck's Germany, and at least once, at the Congress of Berlin in 1878, British Prime Minister Disraeli had to play a complex game of bluff with the 'Iron Chancellor' before Europe's affairs could be sensibly arranged. Additionally, Bismarck's political ruthlessness had made him enemies within as well as outside Germany. He had suppressed opposition and kept a firm hand on liberal institutions, making the Emperor the centre of German national power and prestige and both figurehead and fountainhead of governmental stability.

This arrangement, despite some setbacks and passing difficulties, was successful until 1888. In that year the old Kaiser Wilhelm I died. He was succeeded by his son Frederick III, who was even then suffering from advanced cancer and died within months, before his liberal ideas and generous disposition could have any effect upon the German outlook. There thus came to the throne, at the age of twenty-nine, Kaiser Wilhelm II; and from that moment the downfall of Germany in the modern world became inevitable. The faults and failings of the German nation—arrogance, uncontrolled emotionalism, technical sophistication combined with political primitivism—which had been held to some extent in check by Bismarck's shrewd realism, were perpetuated and exaggerated by Wilhelm II of the swollen head and the withered arm, as they were still further exaggerated and in fact deliberately fostered by his successor Adolf Hitler.

Two years after Kaiser Wilhelm II's accession, in 1890, Bismarck was sacked and the course of history in the twentieth century irreversibly perverted. Everything that Bismarck had striven to avoid within the context of his overall *realpolitik*— hostility to Germany upon two sides, France and Russia, aggravation of England, especially by open challenge to British sea power —Wilhelm II by speech and act recklessly invited. In so doing he ensured the eventual conflict that Bismarck had sought to avoid, and with it the certain destruction of the German Empire. The Kaiser died still hurt and perplexed by charges that he had brought about the First World War, unable to understand that no continental power, even the strongest, could afford to make enemies upon all sides and get away with it indefinitely. Bismarck believed that the Germany he had created had reached the limits of her natural boundaries and that further expansion in Europe should be avoided.

Bismarck's solutions of the various European problems were not and could not be final, but they were at least realistic. The Slav problem in the south and east remained, and the gradually weakening of the ramshackle Austro-Hungarian Empire where resistance to Austrian domination on the part of the non-German elements was gathering force brought ever-increasing dangers. But no political solutions are final; they must be constantly adjusted and reorganized. Yet the attitude of Germany under Wilhelm II after the sacking of Bismarck ensured that the worst was made of a bad situation. Added to Germany's growing industrial and technical power which challenged the established economic forces, this made the eventual outcome inevitable. Bismarck, aware of German political immaturity, had said early on: 'Let us heave Germany into the saddle. She will soon learn how to ride'— and if he and his prudently realistic outlook had prevailed, it might have been so. But too soon a kind of megalomania, centred in a psychologically unstable ruler, took charge, and although the root causes were complex and multisided, therein lay the reason, for the German, and with it the European, tragedy and disasters of the twentieth century.

Germany had risen in a brief half-century to a position of wealth and power challenging the greatest not only in Europe but in the entire world. Wise counsels might still have found an acceptable solution; but wise counsel in Germany went out with Bismarck, and combined with general rivalries and suspicions of the period the result was for Germany a fall more ominous and more spectacular than the rise had been. All who in the nineteenth century had foreseen and worked for a strong, prosperous, united and homogeneous German nation in the centre of Europe, and took deep pride in the achievement, saw it crash to ruin, and many lived to taste the bitter fruits.

All this, though it carries some way beyond the immediate point of reference, is relevant to a study of Brahms because it was of central relevance to Brahms himself, and because it helps to show what it was like to be a patriotic German in the second half of the nineteenth century. If one side of Brahms was deep-rooted in the old German life and feeling, going back past Bach, past the Thirty Years War, to the classical Germany of the Middle Ages, the other side of him was very much an inhabitant of the German present and the resurgence of national unity and identity. He was a great patriot, and his admiration for Bismarck was unbounded. Walter Niemann says that Brahms had his three great 'Bs' whom he revered—Bach, Beethoven and Bismarck. He took all that Bismarck said staunchly to heart, and he was in the habit of including a volume of Bismarck's speeches and letters in his travelling-bag. In his music too he honoured and celebrated German prowess with total sincerity and wholehearted conviction, mostly with choral works. As Niemann accurately put it: 'To him love of his country and people, his Emperor and army, were an inward necessity, a matter of the heart. When he wrote patriotic music, it was the immediate reflection of the patriotic emotions and feelings, joys, forebodings, and alarms which were strongly alive in him.' [1]

So deeply ingrained was his German feeling that he would

[1] pp. 162–3.

quarrel even with his closest friends when he sensed any criticism of the nation, its ruler or its arms, as when he fell out with his crony and travelling companion J. V. Widmann, the Swiss poet and editor, over some political altercation centred on the relative values of monarchism and republicanism. Brahms was a confirmed Bismarckian monarchist, in sentiment a bourgeois liberal-conservative representing the strong central core of German thought and feeling of the time. In this, as in his musical ideals, he stood in some contrast to Wagner, who generally tended to distrust Bismarck's pan-Germanism and whose revolutionary fervours took up a good deal of his time and cost him more than once exile from a German state.

Creative artists tend to be politically naïve, even when they are most deeply committed to specific causes, and neither Brahms nor Wagner were notable political thinkers. But for Brahms, no less than for Wagner, the political movements and affairs of the day were of deep personal concern, and we shall not understand him fully if we ignore or pass by that aspect of his private affairs. His love of German popular life, symbolized by his immersion in both German folk-song and the old German forms of vocal music, was directly related to his contemporary patriotic fervour: the two are inseparably interlinked, and each took the particular form it did, as well as the immediate relationship between the two, largely because of the particular conditions of German national renaissance during his lifetime.

In his later years, Brahms always regretted that he had not in youth done military service; and he tended to envy his young colleagues who went off to join the army. His early romantic dreams which, in accordance with the close connection between romanticism and nationalism, were national as well as emotional, though probably less consciously so, led him to acclaim military glory and feel genuine pride in German military prowess. Destiny led him in another direction; but if it had not, or if he had been born a decade or so later than he was, he would assuredly have take his place in some German regiment of the line. The world might then have exchanged a great composer for a good soldier, and the bargain would not have been a fair or advantageous one;

but either way, this too sheds light and illumination on Brahms's innermost personality.

If Bach preserved the inner German life during a period of national fragmentation and loss of identity, Brahms may be said to have preserved and perpetuated the inner German bourgeois life in the period of national resurgence and triumph. And if Bach's preservation of that life was largely upon the religious plane and Brahms's upon that of restrained romanticism and sceptical agnosticism, that too was in full accordance with the condition and temper of their respective ages. And both were essentially Lutheran-Protestant based, though from opposing standpoints. For Bach's music Brahms had a lifelong reverence, inculcated first by his youthful studies with Marxsen, but also natural and spontaneous.

The rediscovery of Bach, initiated by Forkel's biography and the practical advocacy of Mendelssohn, was a major force in German music during the nineteenth century, an inspiration to all musicians, and to Brahms as potently as to anyone. For a variety of reasons Bach's music had lain virtually unknown and unappreciated for around eighty years after his death; but its re-emergence in the early part of the century came with the force of revelation. Brahms himself was one of the subscribers to the Bachgesellschaft Editions and one of those who truly understood the importance of that immense but not always wisely handled undertaking.

For Beethoven, as for Haydn, Handel was the greatest of all composers; neither knew a significant amount about the great Bach. For Brahms it was different. Whenever a new volume of the Handel edition reached him Brahms would say that it was interesting and he would look into it when he had time; but when a new volume of the Bach edition arrived he would lay all else aside and go straight to it, because there was always something to be learnt there. It was indeed true for him that the completion of the Bach edition and the founding of the German Empire were the two most important events of his lifetime.

Beethoven he worshipped as a musician; but although he has been seen as the heir and descendant of Beethoven, Brahms's natural temperament and musical inspiration were not of that order and lineage. There are echoes, and more than echoes, in plenty, of Beethoven in Brahms: you can find them all through in concealed as well as in obvious places. Yet Beethoven, coming out of the Viennese classical period musically, and out of the Europe of the French Revolution emotionally and intellectually, was only upon some superficial plane the legitimate musical predecessor of Brahms. To find Brahms's true musical roots, one needs to by-pass Beethoven, and Mozart and Haydn also, and go via Bach to the old historic, tenacious Germany translated, paradoxically maybe, into post-Beethoven musical terms.

In one sense Bismarck was to Brahms what Napoleon around the turn of the century was to Beethoven. If Brahms never saw through and became disillusioned with Bismarck as Beethoven saw through and was disillusioned with Napoleon, that may not be entirely from a less penetrating insight. The conditions were very different, and while Napoleon as liberator turned into Napoleon as tyrant, Bismarck remained stolidly and unchangeably Bismarck from beginning to end. Yet a certain correspondence and affinity remain: Beethoven was a Napoleonic composer; Brahms was a Bismarckian one. Loosely and generally speaking of course.

Brahms then was a dyed-in-the-wool German composer. More than a 'national' composer in the narrow sense; a universal rather than a 'folk' composer, despite his involvement in folk-song. But a composer who would be so much diminished as to be all but negligible without his German background and immersion. Wagner represented one side of Germanism in the nineteenth century, Schumann another. But Brahms was the most comprehensive representative in music of the total German consciousness. It is well perhaps that he died when he did, aged sixty-four. If he had lived a longer life, to a little beyond his eightieth year, he would have seen the opening of the European tragedy that was to bring his beloved Germany down in ruin. Though by no means uncritical of German faults and foibles, he would hear no word against the German State and Emperor, even the young Wilhelm II, because he was Emperor.

Brahms's innate conservatism was a product of the times in

which he lived coupled to his social stratum and an inborn bias of temperament. He has been much misrepresented, and maybe he at times misrepresented himself. The comparison with Beethoven is the most misleading of all; and that too he helped along, leaving false clues both internal and external. Towards the end of his life he was inclined to speak slightingly of his own achievement, dismissing it as of small account. He was wrong there, though in some respects not so far off the mark as some of his early adulators would have had us believe. And there are some today who would agree with him wholeheartedly. But we need not concern ourselves too much with the exaggerations and stupidities of either the *ancien* or the *nouveau régime*. There has been too much of that through the years.

He himself would have been appalled to think that in the 'three Bs' his own name would be substituted for that of Bismarck. His patriotic sense would have been deeply affronted. But music lasts longer than politics, and the substitution is just so far as it goes. The fact that the 'three Bs' idea is something of a nonsense anyway lets everybody off the hook, Brahms himself not the least.

The time has come for a new and contemporary analysis of precisely who and what was Johannes Brahms, in historical perspective and in the light of our modern thought and experience. That of course is the general as well as the specific task of all criticism. With Brahms it is especially pertinent because there is still no unanimous consent not only about the value of Brahms's music, which is usual and inevitable, but about the exact nature of it. He may not be unique in that, but he is to say the least unusual among major composers.

2 The Evolution of Genius

He was born of solid Low German stock, on 7th May 1833, in the city of Hamburg. He first saw light in a tiny room at No. 24 Schlütershof (later No. 60 Specksgang) in the area of old Hamburg known as 'Gangeviertel'. Saw light I say; but in fact it can only have been a little light, for those old streets were cramped, narrow, claustrophobic, and the house where Brahms was born a crowded tenement, as we should now call it. Poverty was the lot of the infant Johannes Brahms and his family, though not destitution. They made do, father and mother and two infants (a third, another boy was born two years later, as the sister had been two years earlier. Already Brahms's penchant for the middle course and place was asserting itself).

Some diversionary play has been made with the possible origin of the name 'Brahms'. Some have seen the derivation as from 'Bram', one name for the yellow broom or *planta genista*, the Plantagenet flower common in the low countrylands and the mouth of the River Elbe. This too has been associated with the

16

English 'bramble' and thus taken as appropriate to the thorny
character of Brahms in later life. Is this an emblem of my prickly
nature?' Brahms is reported to have asked the child who handed
him a bunch of dog-rose, according to a story told by Peter Latham
as passed down by Paul Wittgenstein. It looks all very pat, nature
giving him a right name as history set him down in the right time
and place; and it hardly matters now, though it deserves maybe a
passing mention and is in any case preferable to the idea that the
name is derived from 'Abrahams' or 'Abrams' and that therefore
the composer had Jewish ancestry, which is palpable nonsense,
though again it matters little and casts no light anywhere.

Yet natural and historical accident do seem to have played some
small combined part in the formation of Johannes Brahms. If the
name suggests, through some aspect of wild flora, a mingling of
sweetness and thorniness, that is, as will turn out, no way at all
from the true nature and character of Brahms; and in selecting
the city of Hamburg as his birthplace he also showed a kind of
instinctive wisdom and rightness. For Hamburg was one of the
only two important German cities not occupied by a hostile army
during the Thirty Years War—and the other was Vienna where
Brahms subsequently lived and worked for the major part of his
adult life. Indeed, part of the cause of the overcrowding in the
part of Hamburg where Brahms was born was due to lack of space
within the city walls, and these themselves in part had come into
being between 1615 and 1625 when the burghers of the town had
resolutely fortified it against hostile forces and the intrusion of war
into their prosperous lives.

It was largely because of these fortifications that Hamburg
escaped occupation during the religious wars, though in the Napoleonic ones the position was different and Hamburg was taken into
French territorial department. Hamburg was also one of the
Hanseatic Free Cities and one with a particular pride and independence. Its reputation in those respects had lasted well into the
modern period, for when Widmann quarrelled with Brahms over
the political matter, Widmann in some distress wrote to the poet
Gottfried Keller, and Keller's reply contained the significant
sentence that 'the very son of a free town clings more pathetically

to emperor and dynasty than probably ever was the case in the days of former greatness'. Brahms himself fell out with his native city, but was reconciled in his later years and offered the freedom, for which occasion he composed some appropriately weighty and mayoral motets.

Hamburg and Vienna; these were the two centres of Brahms's life. Italy and Switzerland claimed him often for vacation and pleasure in the summer months, but Brahms never took pleasure all that lightly and his vacations were seldom from work, so that his travels and sojourns abroad invariably produced, either at the time or later, music of quality and excellence. He never did visit England, though efforts were made to bring him, and once, when Cambridge University at the instigation of Charles Villiers Stanford offered him an honorary doctorate which required his personal attendance, very nearly succeeded. But cautious Brahms backed down at the last moment, whether because he hated the sea or because he feared some intrusion into or public rape of his cherished privacy is not properly known. But he should have made it to England: he was greatly admired by English musicians, widely influenced them as they tried to restore the vitality of English music, and in general was temperamentally in sympathy with the English mind and temperament, as they with him.

After one childhood temptation and aberration, there seems never to have been any question of Brahms visiting the United States, as did many musicians, among them Dvořák, Tchaikovsky, Johann Strauss. Maybe he would not have found America so congenial, its brash self-confidence and vigorous optimism out of step with his ingrained restraint and subjective melancholy, though the large German immigrant population of the States must have struck a sympathetic chord in him. No matter: he did not go and seems not to have wanted to go.

Brahms was born into a reasonably musical environment. His father was a professional musician of competence if no marked distinction. Brahms's father thus resembled Beethoven's father in one respect, though in all others he was markedly different, being honest, hard-working, good-natured, not clever but straight-forward and dependable, in some contrast to Beethoven's perhaps more gifted but rather feckless male parent. Jakob Brahms played the double bass, and if he was no Dragonetti he managed by diligence and application to make a modest living and to rise a small way in his profession. He also played the horn, and maybe this is where the young Johannes first acquired his love and understanding of that instrument. But the double bass was the father's true and cherished means of making music, and he appears to have treated it as a kind of ally in his struggles with the world, and at times even an *alter ego* when he had differences of opinion with conductors. Anyway, Jakob Brahms seems to have realized his mild ambition to become a reliable orchestral musician and to take his place in Hamburg's musical life.

Brahms's mother, Johanna Nissen, whom Jakob married in 1830, was seventeen years older than her husband and had no musical pretensions, but she was skilled with needle and thread, a shrewd and prudent housekeeper and in most ways an admirable companion for Jakob. She was also a devoted mother who despite hardship and poverty made a good and happy home for her family. Brahms himself adored and honoured her until the end of her life. Although, by the time Johanna Brahms died in 1865, she and Jakob had parted, her death hit Brahms hard: he hurried from Vienna in response to a message from his brother, but arrived too late to see her alive; he enshrined her memory in part of the *German Requiem*. Here again is a small parallel with Beethoven, who also hurried from the Austrian capital to his own dying mother's bedside and whose love for and memory of her left a deep impression on the rest of his life. Also, Brahms like Beethoven felt a strong family responsibility for sister and brother (neither of whom did well in the world), though less ferociously and in rather different circumstances. His sister, Elisabeth Wilhelmine, tended to be wayward and was something of a trial to Brahms for years; but with typical German family loyalty he tried always to guide and helped to support her, though she made an unsatisfactory marriage and did not live up to his own high standards.

The brother, Friedrich Fritz, had promising musical gifts but lacked Johannes's strength of will and character and so, despite firm encouragements, never made anything notable of them.

Maybe delicacy of health had something to do with it and can be advanced in extenuation of his failure to realize his true potentiality. He too studied with Marxsen, and after a period abroad settled in Hamburg as a competent and quite successful piano teacher. If Brahms harboured, as he did, lofty ambitions in music for his brother, they were to be disappointed. Nor was Fritz willing in later years to contribute to the support of their father, which did nothing to foster brotherly love and respect, so that it was not until Jakob's death in 1872 that some reconciliation took place.

Johannes's musical abilities revealed themselves early. He was destined from the beginning for a musical career, following in his father's footsteps. Jakob Brahms had no idea at first that he had bred a musical genius: he simply wished his son to make a modestly competent career in music as he himself had done. But he was a perceptive man and very soon saw which way the wind was blowing. As soon as he took the boy in hand, Jakob Brahms understood that he had no ordinary infant. Little Johannes at once showed an instinctive knowledge of what music was about, way beyond anything he had been taught or at that age could be taught. Jakob expected his son to learn an orchestral instrument with a view to taking his place in one of the local orchestras. But Johannes stamped his small foot firmly down and demanded to be taught the piano.

Jakob did not put up much of a fight and in 1840, when Johannes was seven, took the boy to Otto Cossel, a renowned Hamburg piano teacher. Still Jakob Brahms foresaw only a modest musical career for his offspring, despite the unusual gifts already revealed, and to Cossel he said: 'I wish my son to become your pupil, Herr Cossel. When he can play as well as you it will be enough.' Strange words; but Cossel took the boy on, and with that decision the first big step in Brahms's musical career was surmounted.

Here the youthful Brahms was more fortunate than the young Beethoven had been. Where Beethoven's first teacher, Tobias Pfeiffer, had been a sound musician but a cruel man and a bully, Cossel was at least as good a musician and in addition a kind, imaginative man who quickly established a relationship of trust and affection with his new charge. To Cossel Brahms owed much, and he honoured the memory of his first teacher until the close of his years. Cossel saw at once what manner of talent had come to him, and undertook the boy's instruction with a genuine and humble sense of responsibility, a sense that in a few years' time was to be put to the most severe test and not found wanting.

Outside music, the young Brahms received a moderate but reasonably sound general education at two Hamburg schools. His parents could not afford the best, however much they may have wanted to; but they did all they could. He learnt at his schools the rudiments of essential subjects and acquired some knowledge of French and English. He also learnt to know and love the Bible, as well as the old Protestant church music, under the guidance of Pastor Geffcken of St Michaelis. This too was to have a lasting effect upon his subsequent development. Apart from this, what of most value he acquired from his education, both musical and general, was the habit of application and self-discipline. Throughout his later life he was a determined reader of books by which means he acquainted himself with the best in literature, history and some philosophy. If his formal education was basic and for the most part elementary, firm foundations were laid then upon which he could and did build fruitfully in the years ahead.

But despite the advantages of his boyhood—a happy home life, understanding parents, good teachers—there were other and darker aspects which cannot be ignored, for they too were to have permanent effects upon his character and personality. Poverty was the root cause: because of the constant lack of money, the young Brahms was obliged to undertake disagreeable tasks from an early age. Giving badly paid piano lessons, which he did from the age of about twelve, was perhaps not too severe an imposition. It was drudgery, but many youngsters struggling to get on in the world from a poor background have had to do uncongenial work in order to earn money and help out with the family finances. Though it was boring and uncreative, such work did the lad no particular harm. But it did not end there. From the age of thirteen or so, the boy Brahms was sent out to play at dances and in the taverns of Hamburg's dockland. Here the sailors gathered and the whores plied a lucrative trade. The atmosphere was foul, the language

21

fouler. The pay was minimal but the drink free. If he did not there and then take irreversibly to the bottle, it may well be a tribute to his strength of character. Or it may simply be that he could not stand the taste of the stuff. Either way it was a real danger that, fortunately, he resisted.

But if the physical, and to some extent the moral danger was avoided, the psychological one could not be, and it cut deep. In the Hamburg *Lokale* Brahms made direct contact with the low of sex, and the impact left an ineradicable impression. The boy Johannes not only played the piano but probably sang also in a piping treble (all his life his voice was high-pitched) in the taverns and alleyways of the dock areas. The whores frequented tavern and alley alike, anywhere in fact where the sailors moved or gathered; and few of these ladies of the oldest profession were above using the handsome, sensitive, fair-haired boy to help excite the passions of potential customers. Thus Johannes found himself in all too close proximity to semi-naked (even naked at times) female flesh of no particular sweetness or cleanliness.

The whole business revolted him; and he never forgot. While he played the piano he usually propped some volume of German literature upon the music stand, diverting thereby his attention from the sour and disagreeable scenes around him while he mechanically churned out bad music by ear. He seems to have had from the first that capacity, by no means rare in men of artistic nature and talent, of separating the uncongenial actuality from the free-ranging workings of the imagination.

This is something that can have a number of different consequences. At one level it can enable someone like young Brahms to alleviate an otherwise intolerable situation by keeping the two, actuality and imagination, apart; at another it may well account to some extent at least for the way in which an artist's private life is seldom directly reflected in his works so that a composer does not necessarily write sad music when things go wrong on the domestic front and gay music when all's right in his world. Some do, and maybe Robert Schumann was one; but Beethoven and Mozart are cases which completely demonstrate and vindicate the rule, not by opposing it but through unchallengeable example. The case of Brahms does not here seem to demonstrate either way: some of his private life is in his music, though it is seldom any direct and immediate manifestation; much of it is not. With Brahms it is true that his music was his life. Maybe that is true of any great artist, but with Brahms, whose outward existence was comparatively smooth and uneventful, it appears especially so.

Yet even that may be a partial illusion. An uneventful life, yes; but at the deeper level he too met and had to face the raw edges and harsh realities of human life, as all have to who do not decline the gambit altogether and hide behind some protective shell or artificially erected barrier, either social or personal, and likely both, for the human mind shrinks from the ultimate test and burden of total creative freedom and must cover its tracks at some point or other. Brahms was certainly not guiltless in this respect: he often tried to hide behind something or other; to take evasive action in life and art; to pull down the shutters and turn away from the final clearing of the windows of perception. That is why he must stand always a little below Beethoven who, at the last count, shirked nothing but offered the whole of himself upon the cross of a tragic consciousness. Brahms, after early traffickings with the infinite which turned out to be more apparent than real in the end, was, like his other hero Bismarck, a master of the limited objective and the judicious synthesis.

Brahms's solid North German ancestry is usually held to account for his lifelong prudence and lack of taste for the reckless adventure, whether in art or life. Yet it can hardly have been the sole reason: there have been plenty of wild and wayward characters among North Germans. His own brother showed few of the typically Brahmsian traits. But more than that, more than anything else, Johannes's harsh experiences in the Hamburg *Lokale* while he was still a boy left an indelible mark; caused him never again to take life on trust, especially where women were concerned; taught him to proceed always with caution and circumspection; created in him the beginnings of that reserve which many later on thought to be all but impenetrable, especially if they did not know him well and had not found the way into the concealed and secret corners of his personality. Maybe he was by nature temperamentally biased in that direction anyway, and while he was still young there seems to have remained for some time a certain refreshing openness about him. But his own frequent references to them in later life, often made in bitterness, leave no doubt of the lasting impression made on him by his boyhood chores in Hamburg. And although he lived to become famous and prosperous, his deeper experiences of life only served to confirm him in his habits of prudence and caution.

Yet along with the drudgery of much that he was forced to do, and the salacity of his surroundings in the Hamburg dockland, the results of family poverty and the necessity of contributing something to the household income, fortune also showed him that other side of herself. Cossel was the first example of it; and it was the selfless integrity of Cossel that led him to the second. Already the young Johannes, when only ten years old, had made such strides, his exceptional talents unmistakably revealed and recognized, that there were mutterings in the Brahms circle that Cossel was not pushing the boy on fast enough. Cossel himself knew exactly what he was doing, and for him the only possible other teacher for so brilliant a pupil was his own master, Eduard Marxsen. But Marxsen was not yet convinced, though he did agree, after hesitation, to take Johannes for one lesson a week provided he continued his basic studies with Cossel. For a time this worked well enough. But a private concert was arranged to display the young genius's gifts; and it was a great success, musically and financially, and because of it Jakob Brahms began to scent profit from the gifts of his unaccountably talented son. And this scent was notably sharpened by a travelling impresario who had attended the concert and afterwards whispered in Jakob's ear that much money might be made by taking the lad on a tour of America as an infant prodigy.

Cossel was horrified, outraged. He knew that irreparable harm would come from such a venture for, gifted and progressing fast though Johannes was, the effects of such exposure on a rare talent budding but still unformed filled Cossel with forebodings. Cossel immediately set out to counter the proposal, after violently accusing Jakob Brahms of breaking the promise made when he took the boy on, and as a condition of his doing so, that he should have sole charge of his musical education until he, Cossel, could give no more. Cossel was convinced that for such a pupil, Marxsen was the only possible solution. But if Johannes was to be saved from avarice and exploitation, Marxsen would have to be persuaded to take over entirely. Cossel did not hesitate: without thought for himself and his own reputation he withdrew from direction of his most valuable pupil's musical future and handed him over to Marxsen. Marxsen, the most famous and influential music teacher in Hamburg, firmly knocked the American idea on the head and took Johannes under his formidable wing.

Thus Marxsen became to Brahms what Christian Gottlob Neefe had been to Beethoven. More in fact, for when Marxsen had done his work he had given his charge a comprehensive foundation in musical technique plus a profound and enduring love for and understanding of the music of Bach and Beethoven, so that never again did Brahms need musical instruction but had in him all that was necessary for self-realization. Marxsen was in advance of his time in his appreciation of Bach, whose works were slowly emerging from obscurity, and of the true achievement of Beethoven. Marxsen was a tough and uncompromising teacher, not always easy to get on with but full of understanding and strong in moral as well as musical rectitude. Brahms, always a man of loyalty, never forgot what he owed to Marxsen—or to Cossel, whose personal sacrifice had made the Marxsen advantage possible. Marxsen's part in Brahms's evolution was the more honourable since, knowing the poverty of the Brahms family, he would never take any payment whatsoever for the lessons.

Marxsen's first aim was to turn the boy into a comprehensively equipped virtuoso pianist, a role for which there was already ample evidence of aptitude. Instruction in composition at first played no great part in the curriculum. But Johannes was not to be put off from what he felt rising inside him: already that strain of obstinacy that was to be so characteristic of his middle years was revealing itself. Marxsen, recognizing the inevitable, determined to guide Johannes's compositional ambitions into the straight road of controlled form and musical architecture. Like Beethoven before him,

Johannes Brahms may have begun, and continued, as a virtuoso pianist, but his destiny lay always in the field of composition.

Brahms, even more than Beethoven, is often taken as the case of a slow developer. And in the matter of composition that is basically true, though recent attention to Beethoven's earliest compositions has suggested that he may not after all have been quite so slow to find his true voice as was formerly assumed. In the case of Brahms it is more difficult, for his ingrained prudence caused him to destroy most of the youthful works he did not think fit to publish at the time, and even in later years to consign to the dustbin all that did not pass the test of his ruthless self-criticism. Unless some package of Brahms juvenilia, as yet unknown and unsuspected, turns up somewhere, we shall have nothing new on which to base a reassessment of Brahms's early development beyond what he himself allowed to escape into public circulation; and such a discovery now seems unlikely in the case of Brahms, music's great coverer of tracks. There are a few things of course that have come to light, like the Piano Trio in A minor, issued by Dr Ernst Bucken of Cologne University in 1925 and quite possibly the work played at a private concert given to celebrate the silver wedding of the Schröders in July 1851. But for the most part he ordered his affairs and eschewed loose ends. He no doubt sowed a few musical wild oats; but in the main it is likely that he acquired early and never lost his habit of preparing diligently and prospecting carefully before embarking on voyages of composition, or of doing away with all false or abortive maps and false starts.

Yet if Brahms, upon the available evidence, was comparatively slow to mature as a composer, he exposed his true gifts for music early enough. I think that all creative artists are in fact child prodigies in some aspect or other, and all we know upon the subject must support that view. It may not be true if we measure the prodigy, the miraculous precocity, by the standards of Mozart, or perhaps Mendelssohn; but in the more general and unlimited sense it is a conclusion that cannot be avoided. What sometimes masks the facts in a specific case is that not all infant prodigies are thrust before the public eye, placed upon general exhibition, but are deliberately shielded from exposure and made to follow a more or less 'normal' course through childhood and thus subsequently appear as 'later' developers than those who are, as it were, hoisted to the masthead in short pants and flown there as a kind of battle ensign. Today, when we are much concerned with the effects of child-exploitation, we see less of the infant prodigy and are not so taken with the phenomenon when it does appear; but that does not mean that it does not exist. Also the heyday of the prodigy was broadly speaking that of the Romantic era when childhood was regarded as the glorious period of life, the child God-sent and divinely orientated, possessing wisdom and insights corrupted and ultimately extinguished by the adult world.

Much of this is directly pertinent to the case of Johannes Brahms. He was certainly a child prodigy of the piano and of the musical faculty in general. His precocity was, as we have seen, exploited for gain during his boyhood: that the exploitation took place in the shabby quarters of Hamburg rather than on the public stage of the society world affects the result but hardly the fact. Cossel saved him from the other type of exploitation, and Marxsen kept him at his studies until he was a comprehensively equipped musician. And if he took his time about bursting into the musical firmament with serious composition, that was a matter of temperament and training rather than of innate capacity. He was not precocious in the Mozart way, not the astonishing *wunderkind* in every department of music. But Mozart was music's miracle anyway; altogether unexplainable by any rational or reasonable theory; the nearest we have yet come to the idea of the perfect artist. Brahms, child prodigy at the piano and in musical talent, was nearer the norm for composers; nearer to Beethoven, to Haydn, to Wagner, to most who have come down to us and on whose evolution we have enough information to permit a reliable judgment.

Several factors contributed to Brahms's 'late' development in composition, among them a strong sense of responsibility, implanted in him first by Cossel and then by Marxsen. But was his development in fact so 'late', by regular standards? The idea is open to question. True, he delayed long and prepared cautiously before publishing symphony and string quartet, warned against haste it is said by the example of Beethoven, whose greatness bore upon him and whose path he sought worthily to follow. But that is only the obvious part of the story. He was but twenty years old when he composed and published his first piano sonata, in C, with its direct and unmistakable reference to Beethoven, and the greatest Beethoven of all at that. Neither the music itself nor the gesture behind it suggests either hesitation or timidity. (The F sharp minor sonata, Op. 2, was actually written first; but the two are so close together that both must have come from the same functioning of the creative faculty.) The F minor sonata, Op. 5, also comes from the same years, each following hot upon the other. But the relationship of the C major to Beethoven's *Hammerklavier* is the real pointer. If Brahms waited until middle age to issue his first symphony and his first string quartet because of Beethoven, are we then to assume that he thought less of Beethoven of the piano sonatas than of Beethoven as symphonist or composer of quartets? There is muddled thinking here.

Precocious gifts tend to place a strain on both the physical and the emotional emergence of the child; and poverty places another kind of strain. Young Brahms was a healthy little boy, sturdy enough to cope with the circumstances of his life without much trouble. Yet the complex pressure of strains did begin to tell, though the idea that he never grew to any great height because the poor little fellow was kept out of his bed too long and too often by his duties in the *Lokale* is no more than trivial sentimentality. If it had any effect at all it must have been on his constitution rather than on his inches, yet well into middle age Brahms constantly surprised and frequently discomfited his friends by his endurance on country and mountain walks and by the general robustness of his physique. If he did not grow tall, it was probably just that he was a short man. Increasing girth in later life obviously exaggerated his shortness, but though he may have found it a mild embarrassment at times his lack of tallness was neither the result of insufficient food or sleep, nor a cause of his celibacy, as some have also suggested, he being conscious of it in the presence of taller girls.

At the age of ten he was injured in a road accident, but had no difficulty in recovering. He suffered, we must suppose, the customary childhood ailments; but none left a mark upon him or caused parental anxiety. In 1847, however, the various strains and stresses began to tell. Jakob Brahms, who despite the apparent exploitation of his small son for money, was a kind and considerate father, thereupon asked his friend Adolf Giesemann if the boy might spend a while at the latter's small country estate at Winsen-an-der-Luhe. To this Giesemann readily acceded. The arrangement suited everyone, for Giesemann had a small daughter, Lischen, to whom Johannes would give piano and music lessons in return for good care and country refreshment of body and spirit.

Here was an interlude in Brahms's boyhood with no flaw or distress in it. He and Lischen were soon great friends: as well as making music together they went on long country walks and joined the games of the other children of the neighbourhood. It was here that Brahms, the under-privileged son of Hamburg poverty, learnt to love and understand Nature and the country life. This love was to stay with him, a solace and inspiration, to the end of his days. Though a town-dweller by choice and inclination, he had that deep love for animate nature of all from the Romantic era. A short parallel with the mighty hero again, though Beethoven's love of Nature also included a form of intensely subjective Nature mysticism not in evidence in the case of the more homely and bourgeois-orientated Johannes Brahms. But whatever the bias of it, Brahms's love of Nature was both real and deeply influential on his life and work. And it began here, with the Giesemanns at Winsen-an-der-Luhe, the pert and lively Lischen his daily companion.

In addition to all this, there was an enthusiastic choral society at Winsen; and of course Johannes was drawn to it, preceded by his reputation. He conducted the choir, composed mostly of local schoolmasters and tradesmen, wrote some pieces for them, and generally took his part in their musical activities and some others in the neighbourhood. Adolf Giesemann himself was a keen music lover who could sing well and played the guitar, so during his stay in the country young Johannes was seldom without some musical prompting. Not that he needed prompting, for he was firmly set upon his course and would have sought out opportunities for himself anyway.

Winsen lies between Hamburg and Lüneburg, and every week Johannes made the trip by steamboat to have his lessons with Marxsen at Altona. Sometimes Lischen accompanied him, aided by Adolf Giesemann's brother, who was manager of the railway buffet at Winsen and victualler for the steamboat service. At Winsen itself Brahms and Lischen made friends with the son of a widow who ran a lending library, and through him were able to lay hands on many books which they would read together on country picnics and fishing expeditions. One of these books was the story of *The Beautiful Magelone and the Knight Peter with the Silver Keys*, which hugely delighted the two children and upon which Brahms was many years later to compose a notable song-cycle, after the poet Tieck.

Throughout the summer Brahms and Lischen spent happy days at Winsen, punctuated by regular visits to Hamburg and Marxsen. There is no evidence at all that the relationship between Johannes and Lischen was ever anything but that of good companions: no suggestion that they were childhood sweethearts or anything of that kind. After that first summer of 1847 they continued to see each other for several years; but when Brahms left Hamburg in 1853 for his tour with the violinist Reményi, it was virtually the end of the association. They hardly ever met again, and Lischen married happily not long afterwards. But neither of them ever forgot the summer days of their childhood, and they did keep up some occasional correspondence.

Johannes returned to Hamburg in the autumn to take up his onerous and unrewarding duties again. He was much improved in health and altogether happier and refreshed from his summer vacation. He was able to return to Winsen the next year, but only for a brief stay, for his musical career was now beginning to make significant advances. He still had to attend to his drudge-work; but Marxsen considered him ready to appear in public as a pianist, and he played in concerts in Hamburg in the winter of 1847 and again in 1848. On 10th April 1849 he gave a concert of his own, at which he played Beethoven's *Waldstein* sonata and a Fantasia for piano on a favourite waltz of his own composition, along with various bits and pieces in accord with the popular musical taste of the day. The concert was an artistic success, Johannes's playing of Beethoven and early effort at composition both earning public approbation from Marxsen himself. But financially it did nothing to improve his situation, and the need for money was still the most pressing factor in his life.

If he hoped that concert-giving was going to open new worlds to him he was to be disappointed. For another four to five years he was still to be obliged to continue with badly paid lessons to un-gifted pupils and nightly grinds in the *Lokale* in order to earn a bare subsistence. The effects of such necessity bit deeper still into his mind and character, no doubt emphasized by the glimpse of better things he had thought were to be his after his public début as a concert artist. Many years later, when his fame was high and his position secure, he is reported to have said: 'Few can have had so hard a time as I had.' Although many young composers have had to struggle and suffer poverty and hardship, it was probably true.

Yet, though he could not know it at the time, 1849 was in fact to be the turning point in his fortunes, the destined moment in time when the fresh course in his life was to be finally set. That year saw, as well as his own concert, the arrival in Hamburg of a number of refugees from the abortive German revolution of 1848, among them several Hungarians, and among the Hungarians a spirited and colourful violinist of mixed German-Hungarian-Jewish ancestry whose real name was Hoffmann, but who is known to the world and to Brahms biography as Eduard Reményi. And it was Reményi who held the key to the door through which Johannes Brahms was destined to walk to liberation from the Hamburg life of drudgery and poverty and into the bright world of international musical celebrity.

He was still only sixteen when Reményi first appeared on the scene and his own concert career thoroughly launched—proof enough that his gifts were not unduly slow to manifest themselves, for any boy who could win public acclaim for his playing of the *Waldstein* in those days was assuredly something out of the ordinary. And if the original composition he presented at the same time was nothing special by standards later to be revealed, it still showed from contemporary reports a grasp of form and execution a fair way beyond mere parrot-like competence. He had been hammered into shape by the harsh realities of life, only in part alleviated by the reverse side of fortune's coin. In his case the child was father to the man in a wholly meaningful way. And if the man's time was still not quite yet, the compass point of history was already stamped with his name and insignia.

3 Headstrong Romantic

There are men in history who seem never to have been young; who have come down to us in so fixed an image of venerable years and dignity that it requires an effort of the imagination to conceive that they ever had a youth, still less a youth of passion and impetuosity. No doubt Lord Tennyson and Mr Gladstone were young once, knew the surge of blood and the sap rising, the joys, hopes and despairs of all that youth means and in Nature's sequence must imply. Yet the indelibly preserved impression is one of formidable maturity, hirsutely emphasized. And at first sight it may seem that Johannes Brahms is also of that description. To take a quick mental snapshot of Brahms is to see a man perpetually middle aged, rotund, gruff, the face concealed behind a bush of greying whiskers. And his most familiar music appears to confirm that impression, through its solidity, its prudence, its lack of violent gestures, its immovable sanity, its sturdy moral strength and artistic rectitude. A thoroughly bourgeois music, one might say; and that in one sense would not be very far off the mark. Brahms

33

in his maturity was a representative and accurate reflection in music of the German bourgeoisie of the later nineteenth century at its best, though revealing faults as well as virtues. The middle way of the middle class in an age of strong contrast when national resurgence gave everything a particular twist and meaning. That is the immediate impression; and if, assuming that it is true, it sets him down a rung or two on the ladder, it is always better to see a man as he is than to erect some imposing but ultimately shaky edifice or pedestal upon which to place him, for that way lie only distortion and misconception.

True, the apparent perpetual weight of years such people have to carry is something that belongs to the nineteenth-century Victorian age and image, having also to do with the fashion for voluminous beards. By contrast, the earlier generation of Romantics of the Byron-Shelley-Keats lineage seem to have been perpetually young, and not only because they often died short of years; and from the eighteenth century we have no particular impression of age one way or the other, this also having to do with fashions in dress and appearances of the period. Yet one cannot escape the conclusion that for subtler reasons than appearance some men give the impression that youth was never their natural portion. After all, Wagner, Liszt, Verdi do not leave us with any idea that they somehow by-passed youth, but come to us as men first young, then middle aged and finally old, in the normal and accepted succession.

But of course impression is impression: it is not necessarily the final and irreversible truth. And no matter what may be the case in other examples, Johannes Brahms quite definitely had a youth and went through it with all youth's dreams and heady visions. What is perhaps most remarkable is not the sobriety of his youthful life and music, but the clear evidence in both of forceful exuberance; and if he soon took himself in hand so that by the time he reached true middle age, in years as well as in temperament, it is difficult to believe that intense passion ever did threaten his equilibrium, that still does not negative what was once there.

Exactly why Brahms changed from the impassioned romantic youth of the early years into the rotund, grumpy, reserved middle-aged person of the later years is a question that cannot be answered *a priori*. It was partly due to an inborn bias of temperament; partly a legacy of his childhood experiences in the Hamburg *Lokale* which taught him to take nothing for granted; and partly due to the shattering effects of the Schumann tragedy which confirmed him in his view that life as well as art needed to be handled with caution if overwhelming disasters were to be permanently avoided. It had something to do with the effects of Marxsen's teaching, no doubt, for Marxsen had instilled in him the need for ruthless self-discipline and control of all tendencies towards excess. It had nothing to do with his veneration for Bach and Beethoven, for Bach's music is not basically prudent and circumspect within the context of the times and idiom in which he lived and worked, and Beethoven for all his supreme mastery of form injected new forces of passionate vitality into the art of music. It may, however, have had something to do with an unconscious recognition that unrestrained emotionalism is one of the faults of the Germans, and one likely to upset and distort the delicate balance of the new German nation, and that therefore personal restraint was the correct course for a German composer deeply aware and prideful of race and country. Somewhere, too, there must have been a psychological complication (I hesitate to use the more specific term complex) which drove him back into himself as his general experience of life deepened and widened.

It is an interesting question; and of course in the end a fundamental one. But it cannot be answered by snap judgment or by resort to some convenient turning of fashionable phrase; only through progressive analysis of his developing life and work.

Nor is the matter of Brahms's appearance of perpetual middle age without complication and contradiction. Well past boyhood and into man's estate he was a handsome young fellow, with open features, a finely chiselled face and the look of high spirit and quality. He did not even acquire the beard until 1878, when he was forty-five and had the right to take on a middle-aged look (some put it as late as 1881), and only then because, as he himself put it, 'without a beard one looks like an actor or a parson'. Here again is the call of fashion, for apart from women and schoolboys only actors and parsons appeared persistently clean-shaven, and middle-aged men without a reasonable crop were suspected of being peculiar and lacking in virility. Indeed, to begin with Brahms made of his beard something of a practical joke, disguising himself among friends who did not yet know of the acquisition and deliberately announcing himself as somebody else.

So, from appearance alone, Brahms only became middle aged from his mid forties—which seems reasonable enough. Before that he was noted for his fair hair (flaxen is the word often used), fine countenance, splendid brow and delicacy of build. Later, when he began to put on weight, he gave the impression of compact strength. Only in his last years, his health failing, did he lose his physical power and turn flabby and obviously paunchy. All who knew him before the age of around forty speak of his exceptionally fine head and alert blue eyes. On the other hand, he had no dress sense and actively hated all smart, fashionable or formal attire, so that as he thickened and coarsened he tended to look more and more disreputable. Perhaps he remembered that Beethoven had once been arrested as a tramp in Vienna, and saw no reason why he should flatter the social world with sartorial elegance. He was also very conscious throughout his life that he was a man of the people, of humble origin and allegiance, and so declined to put on airs. It is not of massive importance.

Thus the young Brahms who left Hamburg with Eduard Reményi in 1853 was a slender youth with many fine and delicate features and only a shortage of height to prevent him from being handsome. Nothing here of the portly individual of the later years. Nothing either of the prickly natured, acid-tongued awkward number who often caused offence in Vienna and was not particular if it was held against him. Certainly he was subject to moods, and would sometimes withdraw into himself and decline to join in the general chatter. But all the evidence is that he was friendly, eager, often gay and full of high spirits. Dietrich says that he was 'entirely untouched by the morbid modern spirit'. One side of him was deeply introspective; but he seems to have been quite free from the fashionable breast-beating self-consciousness of the minor romantic posturers. Reményi found him a good travelling companion, as Widmann was to do in after years; and Reményi was not sympathetic to boors and curmudgeons.

Brahms probably met Reményi when the latter was first in Hamburg in 1849. At that time Reményi was en route for America, following the collapse of the revolution. But, like several of his companions, he found the prosperous, welcoming, merchant city of Hamburg a rewarding place to be in and so delayed his exit, taking it has been said some profit from the popularity of farewell concerts. He stayed until 1851, by which time he and Brahms had certainly met and enhanced each other's lives, and then Reményi did make his way to America. But he was back in Hamburg, via Paris, in 1852. This was the signal for Brahms's life to take its new and long awaited direction.

In the spring of 1853 Brahms and Reményi, who had already played in partnership a few times in Hamburg, got together and decided on a short concert tour of nearby towns. They set off in April and gave their first recital at Winsen, where Brahms's friends gave them a warm welcome. Then on to Celle, where Brahms gave a remarkable display of his commanding musicianship by transposing at sight the piano part of Beethoven's C minor sonata, Op. 30, No. 2, into C sharp minor, when they found that the piano was tuned a semitone flat. His colleagues marvelled at the feat, but Brahms himself does not appear to have thought it anything special.

The two young musicians had set out with light hearts and little in their pockets, travelling on foot like a couple of latter-day troubadours. In temperament and personality they presented quite a contrast, Brahms the stocky, sturdy Low German, firm-minded for all his young romantic dreams and aspirations, and Reményi, the flamboyant Hungarian with his taste for *Zigeuner* music and its decorative style and freedom of rhythm and decoration. But they made a good partnership and greatly impressed all who heard them.

The impact of Reményi on Brahms's life was brief but far-reaching. After they parted company later in the same year of 1853, their paths did not cross again. But the association set off a chain reaction that was to carry Brahms far into the musical world so that nothing was ever to be the same for him afterwards. Reményi had known Joseph Joachim when they were both students at the Vienna Conservatoire, and when the pair reached Hanover Brahms met Joachim for the first time, and so began that long friendship which was to last throughout their lives. Joachim, though only two years older than Brahms, was already recognized as one of the leading violinists in Europe. At Hanover Joachim was deeply impressed by Brahms's compositions which Johannes played to him, and he gave the two itinerant recitalists a letter of introduction to Liszt at Weimar. And it was because of these introductions and meetings that Brahms eventually found his way to Schumann at Düsseldorf and so to the key personal and artistic relationship of his entire life. More than that, though Brahms and Reményi were at temperamental opposites, it is likely that it was through his touring colleague that Brahms acquired first that love of the gipsies and their music which was to exert such a happy influence on his compositions throughout his career.

Thus Eduard Reményi appears to have been the instrument of fate that set Brahms upon the path to fulfilment of his rightful destiny. It wanted but a few months of one year to bring about that momentous result; yet during those months the seal was finally set upon the liberation of Johannes Brahms from the circumscribing conditions in which his natural genius had so far been confined, the way ahead apparently blocked for want of free opportunity. No doubt even if Reményi had not appeared on the scene and led Brahms out of the contemporary impasse of his life, he would have found a way out some time. Genius is not to be denied by inhibiting circumstance and, when mind and spirit are strong, will in the end find some way to its ultimate expression. But a decisive push or thrust is often necessary; and in the case of Brahms it was given by Reményi.

Reményi himself was not a man of particular substance or integrity; and when he saw that Brahms rather than himself was winning the plaudits of the musical world, and thus stealing his thunder, he soon determined to rid himself of the encumbrance. At Hanover Joachim had seen which of the two would make a true mark upon the future; and at Weimar Liszt and his companions at once came to a similar conclusion. So after it had become clear that, despite mutual admirations on one level, Brahms and Liszt were musical incompatibles, Reményi saw his chance to ingratiate himself with the Weimar set, declared his allegiance to it, and sent a disconsolate Johannes packing.

Not knowing quite what to do next, Brahms decided to go to Göttingen where Joachim was attending lectures at the university. The two young men spent summer months here in the university town, making music, talking, going to lectures, generally cementing a firm and lasting friendship. If Brahms and Reményi were basic incompatibles, Brahms and Joachim soon found themselves in total sympathy. Joachim had for a short time been attached to the Weimar school of the 'new music'; but he had drifted away, feeling himself not at heart one of them. Brahms himself had been dazzled by Liszt's phenomenal virtuosity at the piano and attracted to Liszt's generous personality. But he too very soon came to the conclusion that the Liszt way was not his way. So between Brahms and Joachim bonds of musical ideal as well as of personal intimacy were swiftly forged, and, apart from the unhappy break caused by Joachim's matrimonial troubles in the early 1880s, they were never to be broken.

Though he had not as yet ventured into publication, Brahms's career as a composer had truly begun and was privately under irresistible way. The earliest piece which was to find its way into his catalogue was the Scherzo for piano in E flat minor, which Liszt played at sight in Weimar, though when it came to arranging a schedule for publication it was placed as his Op. 4 because, as he himself said, one wants to be seen at one's best when one presents oneself first. His best he considered the C major sonata, written after the F sharp minor in strict chronology, though as I have said, these sonatas as well as the more celebrated F minor came so close together that they clearly originated as differing aspects of the same thrust of the creative faculty. Brahms's choice of the C major, parts of which Liszt had also played and greatly admired, to head his published catalogue is interesting. The declaration of allegiance to Beethoven in the opening bars, with their direct reference to the *Hammerklavier* as well as to the *Waldstein* in the structural working

out, was musically a nailing of flags to the masthead, a gesture of
defiance as well as of allegiance, and in placing it at the top of the
list can only have been a confirmation of that gesture.

Yet despite the resounding salute to the great Beethoven fired
by the heaviest guns of the C major sonata, it is very far from being
a species of deliberate imitation—which is not a sincere form of
flattery but mere petty pilfering. Brahms's Op. 1 is in no sense
'written over' either the *Hammerklavier* or the *Waldstein*, a kind
of put-together music by a smart young man who had attended
assiduously to his lessons. If some of the musical devices recall
Beethoven, the voice is unmistakably Brahms. As Wilfrid Mellers
rightly points out, despite the initial resemblances, the effects produced by Beethoven and Brahms are quite different—'Beethoven's
opening bars are an epic challenge: Brahms's suggest a vigorous
bourgeois stolidity, partly because the pace of his harmonic movement confines him to the earth (he has at least two, sometimes four,
chords a bar to Beethoven's one). Similarly, Brahms's modulations
suggest physical energy, whereas Beethoven's hint at mystery—
at the new tonal perspectives which are to be explored in the later
movements.' [1] The poetic content as well as the technique of
writing for the piano are also quite different from Beethoven's. The
resemblances are superficial and openly declared, as they would
not have been if they had not been deliberate but had arisen out
of some unconscious and insidious force of domination. From the
outset Brahms made his position perfectly clear: he intended to
become not the second Beethoven but the first Brahms.

The C major sonata stands in much the same relationship to
Beethoven as on its own ground the First symphony does. But
there is one major difference: when he wrote the C major sonata,
Brahms was conscious only of his innermost responsibility to his
art, determined to honour and uphold those musical values he
judged to be incontrovertible. When he could at last be persuaded,
and persuade himself, to publish a symphony in 1873, however, he
had for some time been manœuvred into a false position in the
quarrel between the 'New Music' of the Liszt-Wagner school and

[1] *Man and His Music*, Part Three, pp. 114–15.

40

those who proclaimed themselves the 'classicists' and upholders of 'tradition'. Thus although there are inevitable emotional and technical immaturities, the C major sonata sounds more spontaneous and less contrived than certain aspects of the C minor symphony, where the conscious onus of living up to the trust of heir to Beethoven obviously weighed heavily upon him.

The sense of frustration, and in parts of impotence, in the C minor symphony were no doubt partly—indeed largely—the result of the Schumann tragedy; but it may also be that they derived from his discomfort at being obliged to uphold one kind of musical composition *against* another. The forceful, sturdy affirmation of homage to Beethoven combined with personal independence of the sonata's first movement has a more potent and authentic ring than some of the pulleys and hoists Brahms uses to assume the mantle of heroic aspiration in the symphony.

There are other aspects to the C minor symphony, most of them as in the sonata having nothing to do with Beethoven; but one cannot help wondering how subtly different Brahms's first symphony might have been if he had never been conscious of the necessity for measuring himself, mind and spirit, with Beethoven, knowing that all Vienna was expecting of him a symphonic work in the direct lineage of the Master, almost a carrying on from where Beethoven had left off in the Ninth. Brahms obliged all right, and the groundlings hailed the 'Tenth symphony'. But one still may ask if it did not go a little against the natural Brahmsian grain, and if that rather than timidity was not the real reason why it took twenty years to come out of the cocoon? The sonatas show that he had ample grasp of form for symphonic composition at an early age; and if lack of mastery of the orchestra is held to have been a stumbling block, then there is every cause to assert that he was perfectly capable of acquiring any musical technique he required any time he needed it.

Point is given to these speculations by the fact that having got the C minor symphony out of the way, he composed his other three with no trouble at all and in pretty quick time. Nor can lack of technique be held to account for his reluctance to produce a string quartet before middle age. Again, it was probably because of the false position in which he found himself as a kind of acting-Beethoven II. Maybe here he was hoist with his own petard to some extent, the result of one of the few acts of indiscretion he ever committed, when he allowed, in 1860, his name to appear on a published paper that was in effect a declaration of war on the school of the 'New Music'.

The C major sonata may abide a fair number of questions; but these are not among them. It is significant too that after the early three he never again wrote a piano sonata, as though here was another direct challenge to Beethoven that must lead him into more dangerous waters. When he wrote his early sonatas, and declared his loyalty in the C major, he was musically innocent and without either acquired or imposed ulterior motives, his reverence for Beethoven spontaneous and uncomplicated. After he had signed the 1860 declaration, he found himself in a hornets' nest.

The F sharp minor sonata, written in 1852 and put out as his Op. 2, offers no salute to anyone or anything but the young Brahms's own emerging genius. There are obvious similarities between the two works: in both, the opening is a strongly rhythmic motif followed by a warmly lyrical one; in both, the second movement is a set of variations on a German folk-theme; and in both, the writing for the piano has an unmistakable feel and stamp. If the latter at times suggest Chopin, or Schumann, or Liszt even, that is largely by coincidence, for at that time Brahms knew nothing of Chopin or Liszt and very little of Schumann. His early provincial isolation in his home city of Hamburg may have had one or two inhibiting effects, but more than these it did enable him to grow up without being confused by a variety of cosmopolitan musical influences. Not that contemporary music was unknown in the Hamburg of the 1840s and early 1850s—only that Johannes Brahms did not hear so much of it and was by training and habit more immersed in the established classics. If his keyboard style had from the outset a distinctly contemporary sound, that was because his exceptional musical faculty was sensitive to, as all such must be, and picked up spontaneously, the prevailing currents of musical thought and feeling.

The F minor sonata, Op. 5, composed in 1853 immediately after the C major, firmly and finally established the scope and quality of Brahms's young genius. If the first two have regrettably fallen into general disuse, the F minor retains its place as the earliest major work of Brahms to be heard with some regularity. Everything about the F minor sonata, including the form with its interpolated 'Rückblick' recalling the theme of the slow movement, proclaims the headstrong, heartwrung, dreamshot Romantic. Yet the logic and intellectual control are remarkable in one so young; and here begins that process of fusion between the lyric and the contrapuntal elements which Brahms inherited from Beethoven and carried on to different ends and other uses. In this way too Brahms set his course clear and direct: all his life he cultivated counterpoint increasingly, and here in the early sonatas' contrapuntal and polyphonic elements is the open declaration of intent. Indeed, Brahms's use of sonata form was never as slavish and seldom as hidebound as his detractors have sought to pretend; and much of his originality lies in his contrapuntal preferences.

Here is both a legacy of and a connection with Bach in German music. Beethoven had resorted to fugue and general counterpoint often enough, and in his 'third period' became a supreme master of polyphony. But for Beethoven fugue and counterpoint were not central principles of sonata form structure, though they were always liable to be contributory. With Brahms it is different: for Brahms counterpoint and polyphonic textures were the staff and grain of musical life, setting him at one with the incomparable Cantor of Leipzig in cast of mind and musical faculty.

Thus the dual aspect of Brahms's creative character was at once exposed. The lyric (represented by song, often folk-song) and the dramatic (represented by contrapuntal and tonal force) may not have been in violent conflict in Brahms's music after the first years, for his temperament was in fact more contemplative and speculative than, like Beethoven's, challengingly dramatic; but the poles of duality are there and can be readily identified, as they must be in all major creative energy, where the ultimate generation comes through interaction of currents, of negative and positive centres of polarity throwing sparks of vital energy across the gap. In these early works, and most noticeably in the three piano

43

sonatas, the duality in Brahms (too glibly defined as that between 'romanticism' and 'classicism') stood out foursquare, perhaps exaggerated by a combination of ardour and inexperience. Later, the relationship was to become tighter and more subtle, less obvious but more all-informing; but not before the most shattering experience of the young Brahms's life had momentarily driven them still further apart.

Though Brahms's early music was firmly based upon classical principles of form and execution, in so far as such principles could be analysed and nailed down in the first place, various other and at the time novel devices appeared in them. The history of art forms seldom divides itself into neat categories and 'movements' for the convenience of critics and commentators, and what may later appear to be self-evident is often only the fabrication of over-tidy minds. Thus Brahms is exampled as the staunch upholder of the honoured classical traditions against the iconoclastic Liszt and Wagner. And even in his time this appeared to be the case. Yet internal evidence does not allow us to play these neat games with a clear conscience, for it takes us behind the façades and reveals to us a good deal that we would otherwise not have noticed or hoped to conceal for our own dark purposes if we did.

If you look carefully into the structure of the early piano sonatas you will find there, in addition to a broad 'classical' structure, clear intimations of the thematic transformation and suchlike, supposedly the property of the satanic Liszt. Some have argued that this was no more than a little of the Liszt influence rubbing off onto the immature Brahms after the visit to Weimar with Reményi in 1853. In fact, however, the F sharp minor sonata was completed before the arrival at Weimar, and most of the C major was in existence by then for Liszt himself to perform. And so close did the F minor follow that it must certainly have been well advanced and almost fully formed in Brahms's mind when he and Reményi took the road to Weimar. Again, as with the sound and texture of the piano writing, these new devices of thematic combination and transformation were 'in the air', part of the contemporary way of using the materials of music in an age of change and expansion. The obvious point that most of these devices, old and new, had been more than hinted at in the later works of Beethoven enhances rather than diminishes the force of the argument. Though it may not be absolutely true to say that there is nothing new under the sun, it is certainly true that nothing exists in isolation.

The relationship between Brahms and Liszt, both musically and personally, is fascinating and illuminating. At the meeting in Weimar there seems to have been a certain reciprocal admiration: on Brahms's part for the superb pianism of Liszt, on Liszt's part for the unmistakable promise shown by Brahms's presented package of compositions. More than that—precisely because of evidences of thematic transformation and the like—Liszt was ready to assume that the young Johannes was a natural recruit to the Weimar circle and its ideals. If this was so, it appears to dispose effectively of the idea that Brahms picked up these new-fangled tricks under direct seduction at Weimar. On the other hand, it is perfectly clear that Brahms did come to the quick conclusion on his own account that the Weimar life and aspirations were not for him. There was no element of propagandist zeal in the decision, for he had not yet met Schumann and so come under the influence of that master's contrary ideals, and was assuredly not at this time involved in the squabbles and rivalries and jealousies of the larger musical world.

Brahms and Liszt were simply incapable of seeing eye to eye in life and art because of a total divergence of temperament. Flag-flying and battle colours had at this time no bearing whatsoever, one way or the other. Liszt's musical outlook and way of life were as different from Brahms's as his private affairs—and one can hardly find a bigger contrast than that. No doubt the earnest Brahms, with his natural reserve behind the youthful passions, detected the exhibitionism, even apparent charlatanism, in Liszt's music and decided that there was not all that much more to it. If so, he was not alone in his assumption. The potent originality of Liszt's musical mind was not yet understood, and indeed was hardly recognized until our own times. The strongly 'moral' and bourgeois side of the nineteenth century, which Brahms had inherited and came to represent in music, was outraged by Liszt's private life and so could see little in his music but an accurate

45

reflection of it. Even today, when we are no longer affronted by the thought of a man who in his youth made triumphal tours with aristocratic mistresses and swept rival pianists off the concert platform with the same ease and flamboyance with which he swept fashionable women into bed, and when the art of music has cleared the range of old smoke-screens, such an attitude is still not dead and decently buried. Hans Gal in his book on Brahms, published first in German in 1961 and in English in 1963, includes the following thoroughly weird paragraph:

Today all this seems strange, considering the fact that Liszt's music, which had produced so much discussion and acclaim at the time and had stood in the very centre of events, has long since vanished from the scene. His greatest works—the oratorios *The Legend of Saint Elizabeth* and *Christus*, the *Missa solemnis* (for a festival in Esztergom, Hungary), and the *Hungarian Coronation Mass*, the *Faust* and *Dante* symphonies—are today only known by hearsay. And if by any chance one of his twelve symphonic poems happens to appear in a concert program, one may rack his brains about why and how such a work could ever have been controversial; nothing of its magnificence is left but trivial, formless, uninspired music of emphatic gesture. Even the once-admired brilliance of orchestral sound—Hugo Wolf declared that he preferred a single cymbal clang by Liszt to a whole symphony by Brahms—is no longer recognizable. This simply proves that sound is nothing but an adjunct to music, and it perishes as soon as the music itself is no longer viable. All that remains of Liszt, the genius who burned himself out like a sky rocket, are a few of his virtuoso and salon pieces and the great fame of a uniquely gifted performer, a stimulating spirit, and a noble, selfless patron of younger artists.[1]

Here is a prime cut of critical inattention and unconsidered special pleading in which any idea of objective truth is swept out with the sawdust. Apart from the obvious fact that Liszt's greatest works, including those mentioned by Gal, far from having 'vanished from the scene' are more widely honoured and understood

[1] pp. 146–7.

Brahms at the age of twenty, by Maria Fellinger, 1853. Frau and Dr Fellinger were great friends of Brahms. Maria Fellinger was a well-known artist and photographer whose later photographs of Brahms became celebrated

Brahms's mother

The house in Hamburg where Brahms was born. No. 24 Schulershof—afterwards No. 60 Specksgang

Brahms at the age of twenty. After the drawing by J. J. B. Laurens, Düsseldorf, 1853. Made at the suggestion of Robert Schumann

The headstrong romantic. Brahms at the time he made the acquaintance of Joachim and Liszt in Weimar during his travels with Eduard Reményi

Brahms in his thirties

The venerable master.
Brahms in his resolute
late middle age

Brahms aged around fifty

Tea in a summer garden

No misogynist. Brahms with
two young ladies, identities
unknown

Brahms in his study at
No. 4 Carlsgasse,
Vienna. Bust of
Beethoven prominently
displayed (this may be
a composite photograph)

Brahms reading in his
library towards the end
of his life

today than at any time since his death, the last part of the paragraph contains enough *non sequiturs* to found a school of paradoxical philosophy, and constitutes, in legal terms, a clear case of approbating and reprobating. For Brahms and his contemporaries of the middle years of the nineteenth century, who saw music from another standpoint, there was no reason to suspect the profoundly original and formative musical thoughts that were to emerge from Liszt's mind towards the end of his life and which were to play an important part in the development of music in the twentieth century; but for the modern critic there is no excuse. Much in Gal's book is perceptive and illuminating; but a habit of making false assumptions undermines too many of the arguments.

That Brahms was dazzled and overwhelmed by Liszt's piano-playing, so different in its spectacular brilliance from his own, is beyond argument, whatever he may have felt about Liszt's compositions as he made their fuller acquaintance during his stay at Weimar. For his part, Liszt understood at once that in the youthful, shy Johannes Brahms a musician of no mean stature was in the making. Liszt was an exceptional man as well as a musical genius, always eager to help young men of promise and quite without personal or artistic jealousy. But if he himself stood above and aloof from intrigue and petty rivalries, there were inevitably plenty of these in an international artistic centre like Weimar. And Brahms, sensing and observing these, appears to have found the atmosphere distasteful. This, added to his lack of sympathy with Liszt's musical ideals, caused the visit quite soon to abort. And it would have done so in any case, even without the unfortunate incident that has gone onto the debit side of Brahms's biography.

The report of Brahms repaying Liszt's kindness and generosity by nodding off while the great man played his own B minor sonata is usually taken as further evidence of Brahms's Teutonic boorishness. Some have argued that the whole story was nothing but a malicious invention of Reményi, irked by the attention paid to Johannes and anxious to wrongfoot him. But the general consensus indicates that something of the sort really did happen. The American William Mason, who was present on the occasion as one of Liszt's pupils and most enthusiastic admirers in Weimar, gave

47

a full description of the affair in his book *Memoirs of a Musical Life*, which Florence May faithfully chronicled in her indispensable biography of Brahms.[1] Even here, though, there is a mild confusion, for Mason admits that he was sitting where he could not at the important moment see Brahms and thinks it was Reményi who told him exactly what had occurred. So it could still have been a Reményi invention. Yet Mason was sure something unusual had taken place, and it may well have been that Johannes dozed through an unguarded moment and was seen to doze by Liszt. Again there is a discrepancy, for the legend is that Liszt stopped playing immediately and left the room, but Mason says that he played on to the end of the sonata before leaving.

It would not matter either way if the thing had not been blown up into a major incident, largely to make a stick with which to beat poor Johannes. If Brahms did sleep while Liszt played, the reason was likely to have been a good deal simpler and less damning than the tribe of detractors and debunkers have asked us to believe. Later in his life Brahms could certainly be churlish, sharp-tongued, careless of his manners; but in youth he seems from reliable report to have been a lad of natural charm and a courtesy that was easily noted but might be disturbed by shyness and a sense of insecurity. Grumpy Brahms belongs to a later time. If he slept at Weimar it was almost certainly due not to boorishness but quite simply to a combination of physical and nervous exhaustion. All his life he was able to drop off for a quick nap whenever he felt tired, any time of the day or night. Probably in his youth he would snooze unintentionally if his constitution needed it, he not having yet achieved control over his physical faculties as he had not over his artistic ones.

Consider: Brahms and Reményi arrived in Weimar after a fair length of travel. For Reményi meeting great men and plunging into high musical society was nothing new. But for Brahms, but recently out of Hamburg, it was something different. He must have approached the house on the Altenburg where Liszt lived with his mistress the Princess Caroline Sayn-Wittgenstein in circumstances

[1] vol. i, pp. 110–12.

48

of considerable splendour, in a good deal of private apprehension. The modest, unpretentious, humdrum middle-class circles in which he had moved in Hamburg were one thing: this place of fame and social as well as musical high life was quite another. When he arrived Liszt asked him to play; but he couldn't face it. Not only would he have had to play to Liszt himself but also to a group of Liszt's notable pupils and colleagues. It was too much. So when he sat down in a comfortable chair while Liszt played the B minor, the tensed-up young Brahms was overcome with mental and physical fatigue and dozed off. Not bad manners: just human frailty.

If in fact he did sleep. Liszt was not in any case a man to bear grudges. Relations between him and Johannes soon began to show signs of unease; but it was not on account of the episode of the kip but because of deep-seated divergences of personal and artistic interest. Without question, Liszt would have helped and encouraged Brahms if the latter had decided to stay on in Weimar and throw in his lot with the prevailing spirit of musical progress there. But it was not to be, and could not be. It was and remained the brief meeting of incompatibles. Other and more appropriate hands were destined to guide Johannes Brahms along the difficult road to mastery and fame.

4 Robert Schumann passim

The year 1853 was a momentous one for Brahms. If it was 1849, though none knew it at the time, when the die was cast it was 1853 which showed the full scope and nature of the casting. Travels with Reményi; Hanover and Joachim; Weimar and Liszt: Göttingen and Joachim again, a friendship consolidated. And still the year was but two-thirds of the way through.

At Göttingen Brahms and Joachim had given a concert which had put a few shillings in their pockets; and upon this advantage Brahms, when he left Göttingen, undertook a tour of the Rhineland to relax mind and body and at the same time to think about his business in the light of all that had come to pass and looked like lying ahead since the April day when he and his companion had taken the road away from Hamburg. He carried in his luggage a letter of introduction and recommendation from Joachim to Robert Schumann in Düsseldorf: it was thus fitting that he should approach the Schumann conjunction via the Rhineland which had such strong associations for Schumann and which Schumann celebrated in his Third symphony, known as the *Rhenish*. For Schumann the banks of the Rhine and the surrounding hills and valleys were something apart and especially meaningful, the city of Cologne with its noble cathedral figuring also in the symphony in memory of a visit Schumann paid there in 1850 for the enthrone-ment of the archbishop, a centre-point, Düsseldorf, where he settled also in 1850, another.

When Schumann had been in Hamburg that same year of 1850, the boy Brahms had sent him a package of compositions; but Schumann was too occupied then to do anything more than return the offering unopened. Brahms does not seem to have been too upset; but the abortive move may have made him initially a little re-luctant to approach Schumann again in a hurry. However, Joachim was already a friend of the Schumanns, and besides giving Johannes his letter of introduction had, upon observing the young musician's quality, immediately written to Schumann also announcing the good news from Hanover. Thus when Brahms, after wandering alone some time through the Rhinelands and finding, again through Joachim's recommendation, warm hospitality with the Deich-manns at Mehlem, presented himself at Schumann's door, he came as no unrecognized and unannounced stranger. The stay with the Deichmanns had been particularly fortunate for Brahms, because hitherto he had not known a great deal of Schumann's music and what he did know he did not all that much care for, but the Deichmanns were great Schumann lovers and by the time he left them Brahms was too, having learned to know and love many of Schumann's best compositions.

The story of Brahms's reception at the hands of Robert and Clara Schumann is well known; too well known to warrant detailed repetition here, for it is not in dispute and has never presented a difficulty. Nor is there any question about the warmth and sin-cerity of Schumann's recognition of Brahms's musical gifts. On the other hand, the fact that Schumann hailed Brahms's genius is no cause of astonishment in itself. It is to the credit of Schumann's generosity and magnanimity of spirit, but hardly to his critical perception for the evidence was so clear, so known in advance, that any other course would have been impossible. Schumann was quite capable of critical insight of an audacious order, as when he hailed the genius of the virtually unknown Chopin upon the slender evidence of an early and not characteristic work; but with Brahms the obvious was so clearly outlined that not to have grasped it would have been a considerable achievement. After all, Brahms's talent and quality had already been recognized by Joachim in Hanover and by Liszt in Weimar, as well as earlier by Marxsen in Hamburg: Schumann's hail and salute were in the nature of confirmation from an admired and influential source.

Since the breakdown of eighteenth-century order and rationalism following the impact of the French Revolution, the arts as well as the politics of Europe had been in the melting-pot. At the extremes, as always in such a situation, it was a clear fight between those who wanted to resist all change at any cost and those who wanted to change everything at any cost. The real conflicts and tensions were of course subtler and less obvious. In music the streams divided not into two but roughly into three. On the one hand was the Leipzig school, who thought of themselves as guardians of the sacred temple, but recently and sadly deprived by the death of Mendelssohn, and who would countenance nothing in the way of innovation and for whom 'progress' was virtually a dirty word. At the other end were the 'progressives' of Weimar, flying Liszt's banner and also that of Richard Wagner. In the middle were those of Schumann's persuasion and cast of mind and temperament.

In a sense the Schumann group constituted the middle way, and in so far as that is true it was natural that Johannes Brahms should take station behind the leader. But it was not quite so simple as it sounds (the 'middle way' never is), and within it were many differing strands and currents. If the Leipzig group would have no progress and the Weimar group nothing but progress, there was a good deal of elbow room round the Schumann banner. The advantage of the middle way or happy mean is that except at the furthest extremes both ends tend to be substantially open: the disadvantage is that there is no immediate 'cause' or clearly defined battle cry and positive objective of the kind which always attracts and is often necessary to the young, especially those with ardent ideals and starry ambitions.

For the strict (as they wrongly thought themselves) adherents of the departed Mendelssohn, the future of music lay in reverence for its past and virtually no deviation from the 'pure' classical principles. To the followers of Liszt and Wagner that same future lay in the overthrowing of all that musical composition had meant in the past in so far as structural cohesions and technical procedures no longer answered to the pressing sense of the new age with its new feelings. For those who enrolled under the Schumann ensigns, neither past nor future was quite so simple as that. In seeking a classic-romantic synthesis they believed that the true way was via established and honoured forms suffused with new feelings via technical means which increased expressive power without undermining inherited formal tradition. To this end they believed that Beethoven had shown the way—and so to some extent he had. But Wagner also believed that Beethoven had shown him the way and justified, in the Ninth symphony especially, his own progressive art forms. Schumann was known as a leading 'Beethovener'; and Brahms was very soon recognized as another. Yet Bach was the great inspirer also for the Schumann school, as he had been for the Leipzig party under Mendelssohn (after all, Mendelssohn himself had been one of the prime movers in the rediscovery and re-honouring of Bach, at Bach's own *Gewandhaus* in Leipzig). And the Liszt-Wagner alliance also honoured Bach.

So it seems clear that however harsh the splits and divisions may have seemed at the time, or how much bitterness these passing quarrels engendered (and they were to get worse before many years were out), or how much interested parties may have laboured to perpetuate them into later ages, there was considerable interaction and cross-referencing, though many involved at the time and after would have taken their lives rather than admit it. Probably even in ages of disruption and violent change, it is true as Bartók said that in art there are only slow or fast developments, essentially evolution rather than revolution. In the middle of the nineteenth century it seems that evolution was proceeding at several different paces at the same time.

The pivotal middle course suited Schumann's temperament and outlook. There is good reason to see Schumann as the quintessential poet in music of German Romanticism, the musician who was closest in spirit and sympathy to the Romantic poets and novelists of the period—Novalis, Jean-Paul Richter, E. T. A. Hoffmann. There was nothing in him of the all-or-nothing, hell-and-high-water recklessness of the Wagnerian or Byronic High Romanticism; but he dreamed the inward Romantic dream and became its leading spokesman in musical terms. This side of Romanticism was rooted in the domestic, bourgeois, middle-class German life, and here again Schumann with his happy family life and firm domestic loyalty was among its foremost representatives. Schumann's creative imagination was freed and inspired from various sources—contemporary poetry and literature, reverence for the classical masters of music, love of wife and children, instinctive feeling for homeland and people.

Into this contented but active home came the young Brahms. He found there the kind of private and musical life he had not previously encountered. His own home life, though happy, was tainted always with hardship and poverty and thus too inhibited for a young man of burgeoning dreams and ideals. And at Weimar everything was pitched at too high a level of artistic and social extravagance to appeal to his own solid North German temperament. But with the Schumanns at Düsseldorf he felt immediately at home in totally congenial company. The effect of that encounter was to bend irreversibly the entire course of his life.

For one thing it brought him the first sight of Clara Schumann, that stalwart woman and internationally famous pianist who after Schumann's tragic death three years later was to work with devoted loyalty in honour of his memory with as much determination but less autocratic obstinacy as Cosima Wagner was later to labour on behalf of her own dead husband's interests, and who for Brahms until the end of their joint days was to be beloved over all.

Musically, the meeting with Schumann was to have hardly less far-reaching consequences. Immediately Schumann saw in the young Johannes a fellow spirit of unlimited promise and the brightest of bright hopes for the future of German music. 'This is he that should come,' Schumann declared in a letter to Joachim soon after Brahms had arrived with his potent music. Schumann at once began to arrange for the publication of Brahms's works by the Leipzig firm of Breitkopf & Härtel. Encouraged by Schumann's recommendation, the famous publishers were very willing to include Brahms's early works in their lists, and issued them in the order desired by the composer—the two piano sonatas and the Scherzo, plus a collection of songs put in as Op. 3. At the same time another publisher, Bartholf Senff, published a further set of songs and the F minor sonata, Op. 5. These were not the only works Brahms had under his belt; but a Fantasy Trio and a string quartet failed to get past his rigorous faculty for self-criticism and were destroyed, and a sonata for violin and piano, intended for Senff, was lost, whether by Schumann or by Brahms himself is not clear.

But this is to anticipate a month or so. At Düsseldorf Brahms was soon on terms of the closest friendship and intimacy with the Schumanns. If he was boorish and awkward, there is no record of it here, and no suggestion that he ever allowed a disagreeable impression of himself to show to Robert and Clara. They loved him and he loved them from the outset.

Among the members of the Schumann circle was the young Albert Dietrich, who was many years later to write a revealing account of Brahms between the years 1853 and 1874, from which it is again clear that in youth Brahms was both likeable and well liked, serious but by no means solemn, and good company at home and on expeditions. Despite his reputation for grumpiness and bad temper in later life, Brahms always had the capacity to make and keep staunch friends; and here in Düsseldorf he revealed that capacity early on.

Brahms stayed with the Schumanns from September until early November 1853. In addition to Schumann's constant and valued advice in composition, and the growing personal affections, there had been the diversion of the F-A-E sonata, written in honour of a visit by Joachim (who had adopted the words *Frei aber einsam*— 'Free but solitary'—as his personal motto), a movement each for violin and piano composed by Dietrich, Schumann and Brahms.

Joachim came, was asked to guess who had written what, did so without the slightest difficulty, and everybody enjoyed the prank. The MS. was later in Joachim's possession, and he did not allow any but the Brahms movement to be published, believing that the Schumann contribution in particular was below standard. But the whole was eventually issued in 1938. This small incident was not of great importance; but it does help to indicate the happy, carefree, uncomplicated atmosphere then prevailing in the Düsseldorf circles.

But if the F-A-E sonata business was a diverting *jeu*, Schumann's next move was something entirely different. On 28th October there appeared in the *Neue Zeitschrift für Musik* Schumann's unprecedented eulogy of the so far still virtually unknown Brahms, under the title '*Neue Bahnen*', or 'New Paths'.[1] This set the entire musical world by the ears: established composers sat up and demanded who was this Johannes Brahms, while aspiring ones felt that so eminent and influential a championship had given a rival an unfair and largely unwarranted advantage. Since jealousy is a strong force of human emotion, many were set against Brahms for no better reason than that, being launched in such terms by such a master, Brahms had been guilty of collusion and had jumped the gun. But by no means everyone held it against Brahms that he had come so fulsomely under fortune's star. Indeed here began that overt cleavage in the musical world which was to cause so much dissension and so many barren quarrels in the years to come. Obviously Schumann himself had intended no gesture of division: he had become convinced of the young Brahms's unique quality and wished only to bring the glad news to a musical world not at the time overburdened with genius sympathetic to his own ideals. Schumann was ailing by 1853, becoming more and more aware of the symptoms of mental and emotional instability that were soon to overwhelm him; and it is possible—more, it is likely—that the sense of his own declining power caused him to hail in particularly joyous terms one who he believed would carry the banner into the future. That in so doing he should have driven wedges into the

[1] See Appendix.

56

musical life of Germany—and not only of Germany—would have caused him real horror.

Schumann's reputation as a critic was hardly less than his reputation as a composer. In both respects he was one of the world leaders, and had been for twenty years. He had founded the *Neue Zeitschrift für Musik* in 1834, and remained its editor, proprietor and principal critic for ten years. He had relinquished it in 1844 when he moved from Leipzig to Dresden and turned it over to a colleague. Since then it had tended to move, not to his own pleasure, to the Liszt-Wagner 'neo-German' camp, and when he wrote the 'New Paths' article he had not contributed to its pages for a decade. Indeed, he had not published any criticism for around four years, so his new and unexpected pronouncement carried more weight and produced a greater effect in consequence. During his years of editorship of the *Neue Zeitschrift* Schumann unquestionably revealed himself as a great critic; and declining health did not reduce his innate powers of perception. He was not infallible—no critic is, or can ever expect to be—but he was unfailingly generous, high minded, truthful, quite without jealousy or petulance. He wrote out of love for his subject, not from incurable hatred of it, as many who address themselves to the critical task appear to. If ever there was one who justified Frank Harris's dictum that a great reviewer should be a star finder not a fault finder, it was Robert Schumann.

Oddly, Schumann did not tell Brahms about the 'New Paths' article, leaving Johannes to discover it for himself, which he did in early November, by which time he had left Düsseldorf and was back in Hanover at the behest of Joachim. Brahms's private feelings on reading the Schumann eulogy are not recorded. He would not have been half human if he had not felt a swelling pride at so handsome a tribute from so honoured a source. But he would have been a fool if he hadn't felt certain qualms at what the immediate result might be for him, and realized that as well as a heart-warming gesture of support Schumann had laid a heavy burden on his young shoulders. He must surely have known that one way or another there was bound to be an uncomfortable backlash.

Heavy burdens on the shoulders, however, were nothing

markedly new for Johannes, and certainly nothing to worry him overmuch. Schumann occasionally overrated a mediocre talent, as all critics do who are motivated by generosity rather than malice; but in the case of the young Brahms he spoke true. Schumann himself must have known that he was on target in this case; and Brahms must have known it too, however momentarily uncomfortable the publication of such a panegyric and its immediate consequences, for though there are instances of the contrary, in a general and reliable way of speaking genius is conscious and aware of its powers, and will be especially so in youth. The direct result of Schumann's eulogy was to make Brahms stiffen his resolution to uphold the honour and dignity of the art of music, both as composer and executant, and to reinforce his already formidable shield of ruthless self-criticism. Such praise from such a master might easily have gone to the heads of some young men; caused an upsurge of natural vanity which could have led to disastrous consequences later on. That such was the last thing likely to happen to twenty-year-old Johannes Brahms is but another tribute to his steadfast character and unshakable integrity.

Here again we may pause to consider the physical appearance of Brahms at the age of twenty in this key year of 1853, as further counterblast to the idea of him as perpetual middle-aged grump. The visual image is preserved in the pencil sketch by J. B. Laurens, made at this time; the verbal one by Dietrich, who wrote: 'The appearance, as original as interesting, of the youthful, almost boyish-looking musician, with his high-pitched voice and long, fair hair, made a most attractive impression on me. I was particularly struck by the characteristic energy of the mouth, and the serious depths in his blue eyes.' And a page on, writing of an excursion to the Grafenberg: 'Brahms was of the party, and showed himself here in all the amiable freshness and innocence of youth; pulling turnips up from the fields, and cleaning them carefully, he playfully offered them to the ladies as refreshment.'

Revealing details—and there are many more. Whatever he may have become, either deliberately or through the pressures of life and its experience, the young fair Brahms who visited the Schumanns in 1853 was anything but a churl and a boor. Only a want of height and an ingrained shyness apparently prevented him from being hailed all round as a young god, some golden Apollo but recently decended from Olympus for the solace and inspiration of a sorely tried world. Maybe that is another kind of exaggeration; but inasmuch as the young Brahms has been largely lost behind the beard and the brusque manner of the succeeding years, it is well to remember that it was not always like that; and indeed it might never have been quite like that had it not been for the overwhelming disaster, the heart, mind and soul shattering tragedy about to be enacted upon the stage of his inner and outer life.

Signs of Schumann's ailment had been discerned for at least a decade. Exactly when they first appeared is difficult to assess; but certainly in 1844, with the return to Leipzig after Clara's successful tour of Prussia and Russia, the telltale symptoms were more than hinted at. That was when he gave up the *Neue Zeitschrift* in order to conserve his energies as much as possible and to concentrate on composition. His outgoing force put into his music, though, overtook his now slender resources, and led to another breakdown. A life kept on an even keel, and the constant solicitude of family and friends, enabled Schumann to continue with work for a number of years. In 1850 he moved to Düsseldorf as music director. Though he held the appointment until his final breakdown and attempted suicide in 1854, it was not the success he and Clara had hoped for when they moved from Dresden and found a warmth of welcome awaiting them in the old Rhineland city.

Schumann was not a particularly effective orchestral and choral conductor, for he was at once too unassertive a character and too subjectively immersed in the music before him to make the best of singers and players not always highly expert or markedly attentive. Discontent began to rumble as early as the end of the first season and it soon became evident that despite his reputation and prestige, and for all Clara's loyal support, he was quite simply not the man for the job. Maybe if his health had been better, his mental force more reliable, it would have been different; but that in the end is but an excuse, for the truth is that the gentle, reflective, daydreaming Schumann was not cut out for any official position in musical affairs, and certainly not for a major post in conductorship,

59

with its requirements of a combination of some sense of self-dramatization and a capacity for decisive leadership. The successful conductor does not necessarily need to be an exhibitionist or a martinet; but he does require certain definable qualities which were not by nature or aptitude Robert Schumann's. He was the subjective poet, the romantic dreamer of romantic dreams; and when he conducted he tended always to lose himself in the beauties of the music as it sounded in his own mind, unconcerned about the quality of the actual performance, or, if report may be believed, actually at times unaware if it went utterly wrong and distorted.

How much these attributes of Schumann were inborn and congenital, and how much due to the failure of his health, it is hard to say. But it does seem clear that towards the end, during the later Düsseldorf years, Schumann became more than ever introspective, more withdrawn into himself, and ultimately more tormented by wild fancies than ever before; and no doubt this affected his work on the rostrum as well as at his desk.

Not that it affected his critical judgment: indeed, it may well have been sharpened by Schumann's subconscious awareness that his own time was short and that someone else must carry on the work he had done and devoted his best years to doing, through criticism as well as in composition. Schumann's later music, though it is often dismissed as the enfeebled production of an ailing mind, is by no means all below par, and some of it shows distinct advances in technique and gives clear evidence that if Schumann's mental health had not been fatally flawed, his ultimate contribution to the evolution of music in the nineteenth century would have been even more potent than it was, probably running parallel with that of Brahms in the sense of taking a similar direction from a slightly different point of emphasis.

Schumann, profoundly influenced by the art of Bach—his well-known remark, that it is hardly too much to say that music owed as great a debt to Bach as Christianity owed to its founder, makes his faith in that respect abundantly plain—was no less thoroughly versed in the art of Haydn, Mozart and Beethoven. Thus, though his precise musical faculty differed from that of Brahms in several important respects, and he never developed Brahms's strong intellectual command of form on the largest scale, both the past and the present allegiances and ideals were very similar. No doubt that is why the great sympathy and mutual understanding grew between them so quickly and so comprehensively.

But, whatever Schumann in full possession of his health and faculties might have contributed to the continuing nineteenth century, it was not to be. Some malformation of the skull, causing protrusions to grow on the inside and press progressively into the tissue of the brain, cost him first his health and reason and eventually his life at the early age of forty-six. The twin aspects of Schumann's genius, the Florestan and Eusebius division, need not be taken as evidence of incipient schizophrenia. It may well be that like many of the Romantics, like Liszt in another sense, he was a dual rather than a split personality which, but for the physical aberration, would have been vitalizing instead of disintegrating.

The existence and provenance of Master Raro, associated with Friedrich Wieck, father of Clara, in the activities of the secret and imaginary '*Davidsbund*', holding the balance between Florestan and Eusebius, indicates that there was no decisive and irrevocable cleavage and that the internal relationships in Schumann's mind were quite consciously and deliberately, even half-humorously, maintained. All the same, there is evidence of imbalance and potential instability in Schumann's personality from the beginning. His habit of concentrating upon one type of composition at one time—piano music for a year or two, songs for another brief period, then symphony, and chamber music next—appears to indicate that there was little of that cross-fertilization which proclaims the whole of the creative faculty functioning healthily and productively all the time. There is often some tendency for genius to apply itself naturally and without conscious deliberation to one aspect of work in a certain period—Haydn, Mozart, Beethoven, Brahms himself, appeared to work predominantly in a particular direction at a particular time—but it was always inclusive, never exclusive; certainly never, as with Schumann, almost obsessional, so that there is an inescapable sense of lurching in one direction or another and it becomes all but impossible to define the structure of genius or find the true centre of its unity. How much in Schumann's case this was the direct result of the physical pressures on the brain and how much to some deep-seated psychological dichotomy, or even an interactive combination of the two, is impossible to decide. But the physical damage, increasing with the years, must be seen as the major contributory factor.

Whatever the ultimate truth of Schumann's personal tragedy, the effect on the life of Johannes Brahms was momentous. After staying a while with Joachim at Hanover, Brahms went to Leipzig, principally to arrange for the publication of his works by Breitkopf & Härtel. In Leipzig he again met Liszt, who was in the city with Hector Berlioz upon the occasion of a major concert of the latter's compositions. The jealous rivalries between the various musical parties, partially stoked by Schumann's '*Neue Bahnen*' article, were rife in Leipzig, stronghold of the artistic conservatives. But Brahms seems not to have been in the least put out by such trivial goings on, and on his own part quelled them by his personal charm and modestly unassuming manner. His fresh encounter with Franz Liszt revealed no uncongenial legacy of whatever disagreeable incidents may have taken place at Weimar: Liszt's natural magnanimity combined with Johannes's unpretentious bearing appear to have banished all potentially unhappy memories.

Both Liszt and Berlioz were present when Brahms played the C major sonata at the Leipzig *Gewandhaus,* and the critical reception, though cautionary, was by no means hostile. On the other hand, there was no sign of wild adulation for the young man, and plenty that he was in some danger of being caught between the cross-fire of warring factions. The conservatives warned him against 'over-enthusiastic patrons' and the 'neo-German' progressives were still inclined to suspect him of apostasy. Not for the first or last time a young man, who could not easily be pigeonholed and provided small grist to embattled mills, found himself stranded in no man's land and little understood upon either hand. Here too Schumann's eulogy was working against him, for many of those who had read it were puzzled, expecting a second Beethoven or Mozart and so pitching their anticipations too high. Looking for a new Minerva springing fully armed from the head of

Jupiter, as Schumann had intimated, they found only a richly gifted but as yet not fully matured young man, and began to wonder what all the fuss was about.

Brahms himself took it all with philosophical calm of mind and spirit, not even suspecting yet the wrath to come from Leipzig when he presented his D minor piano concerto there six years later.

By the end of that key year of 1853, Brahms was back home in Hamburg, missing out a projected brief stay at Hanover on the way. The Christmas reunion with family and old friends was heart-warming. His mother was overcome with joy and wonder at the almost fairy-like success story of her beloved 'Hannes'. His father, who had also risen a little in the world during the intervening months and become a double-bass player in the theatre orchestra, enabling the family to move a rung above the poverty line, preened himself with unconcealed pleasure. Brahms too was full of uncomplicated happiness to have been able to make his return in very different circumstances. It is said that he even went round the *Lokale*, where he had played and suffered as a boy, to convince both himself and them that the old ways and necessities were gone for ever. He could have been forgiven if he had felt a sense of cautious satisfaction at the way things had gone for him in a short nine months.

The full and farthest-reaching implications of those busy months between mid April and late December 1853 are admirably summed up by Florence May:

> The journey was the transformation scene of his life. The obscure musician who, having been guarded from the dangers of prodigy fame, had started from Hamburg in April without prestige, without recommendations, without knowledge of the world, its manners or its artifices, had passed from the two or three provincial platforms on which he had appeared as Reményi's accompanist, to present himself as pianist and composer in the Leipzig *Gewandhaus*, and to return to his home in December the accepted associate of the great musicians of the day; recognized by Weimar, appreciated by Leipzig, encouraged by Berlioz and Liszt, claimed by Schumann

and Joachim. Before he had well begun to climb the steep hill of reputation he had found himself transported to its summit. Starting hardly as an aspirant to fame, he had come back the proclaimed heir to a prophet's mantle. His life's horizon had been infinitely widened, his whole experience changed. Back again amid the familiar scenes of Hamburg, the events of the past nine months must have seemed to him as the visions of an enchanted dream.[1]

Hamburg was not only overjoyed but also astonished by Johannes's marvellous success. The honest, friendly, unostentatious Hamburgers of the Brahms circle must indeed have thought it a great wonder that one from among them should have gone forth and taken the big world virtually by storm, as it must at the time have seemed. The more prosperous citizens of Hamburg were quite accustomed to creating a stir in the world; but hardly those of the lower middle class from which the Brahmses came. Only Johannes's old teacher Eduard Marxsen was not surprised. He had always believed in the boy's capabilities and once declared that they would soon compensate music for the early loss of Felix Mendelssohn.

There have been suggestions that Marxsen's influence on Brahms's development were not quite so far-reaching as many have claimed; and indeed Brahms himself is reported once to have said that he learnt nothing from the stern master of his youth. But that was probably in a moment of bad temper, and in any case it is difficult to define the exact nature of the influence of one man upon the early growth of another at the distance of more than a hundred and twenty years. In any case, Brahms more usually referred with affection and gratitude to Marxsen, would not for years publish major works without Marxsen's approval if there was opportunity to submit them for criticism; and most telling of all, dedicated his B flat piano concerto to his 'dear friend and teacher Eduard Marxsen'. That departing gesture from a now famous pupil to a master nearing the end of his life seems fairly conclusive and to overweigh any ephemeral mutterings of discontent or disaffection.

[1] vol. i, p. 153.

History does not appear to have recorded what Cossel thought of his former charge's more or less triumphant return to Hamburg; but it is difficult to think that he was any more surprised than Marxsen.

But the enchanted dream, if such for the young Brahms it really was, did not last. Early in 1854 Brahms went to Hanover again to join Joachim, and also Julius Otto Grimm who had been in Leipzig the previous year and had quickly become a friend of Brahms. These were happy days still for the young musicians, soon made happier by the arrival of the Schumanns for a concert in which Joachim was to conduct Schumann's D minor symphony. Though Schumann was by now dangerously subject to moods and fits of melancholy, and was showing clear tendencies of hallucination in which he believed himself in touch with the dead, the Hanover visit brought him back to his best spirits. During those days there seemed no cloud in the sky, no flaw in the continuity of life's reward and happiness. The concerts went splendidly: the Schumann symphony was warmly received; Clara Schumann played Beethoven's *Emperor* concerto; and Joachim himself played a new written work for violin and orchestra of Schumann which was dedicated to the great violinist. Nothing could have been better, more carefree.

The blow when it fell was thus all the more shattering; a thunderbolt out of a clear blue sky. The Schumanns returned to Düsseldorf at the end of January and Robert Schumann wrote Joachim a cheerful letter dated 6th February from which there could be no possible premonition of disaster. Yet within two weeks all was lost. Schumann began to have severe pains in the head and was tormented by a single note singing in his ears. On 17th February he got out of bed in the night to put down on paper a theme he was convinced he had received from the angels. It was the last thing he committed to manuscript, the now celebrated theme in E flat.

He recovered a little during the next days, but only for brief periods, and became immersed in making variations on his angelic theme. Then on 27th February he left the house during a moment when Clara's vigilance was relaxed, walked to a bridge over the

River Rhine and threw himself into the waters below. He was fished out by the crew of a passing steamboat and returned to his home by carriage. But he was now totally insane, and after a doctor had succeeded in temporarily calming him Robert Schumann was confined in an asylum at Endenich from which he was never to come out. He lived for two more years, occasionally lucid but more often sunk in impenetrable mists of incomprehension, suffering greatly but sometimes too imagining that he heard, and maybe was composing, celestial music.

When the Schumanns left to return to Düsseldorf Brahms remained with Joachim and Grimm in Hanover; and it was there that they heard, incredulous, the appalling news of Schumann's attempted suicide. They wrote at once to Albert Dietrich for news and clarification of the newspaper reports. But Dietrich could not reassure them: all that had been reported was true. The correspondence in Dietrich's *Recollections* fills in the details and conveys the sense of shock felt not only by the intimate circle but by the whole musical world at the tragedy.

What underlying effect this disaster had on Brahms we can only guess at. The immediate impact was obvious; but it sank deeper than that; sank in fact so deep that it certainly affected the whole of the rest of his life, caused him once again to recoil into himself, to build round his life and its sensitivity a belt of armour plating which was to thicken as he grew older and behind which he soon retreated. In later years only now and again, at rare and long separated intervals, did anyone have a real glimpse behind it, outside his music. Even there the reserve is not to be mistaken, the open if sometimes heavy-handed passionate outpouring of the early years was soon put under strong guard. His agony did a few years later find its true expression in music of compelling and anguished power, in the first movement of the D minor piano concerto; but for the most part the blow was mortal to the quiet young man who had begun to find a primrose way in the world after inauspicious beginnings. The enchanted dream was over. It had been brief enough.

The situation at Düsseldorf was dire. Joachim could not leave

Hanover because he held an official appointment there. But Johannes was free to go—and he went, with all dispatch, his mind no doubt a tablet of unutterable thoughts.

Arrived at the Schumann house, he found things all over the place: Clara Schumann in despair—she was pregnant again, for the seventh time—nobody with sense or balance anywhere in sight. The young man acted swiftly, promptly, effectively. Frau Schumann was calmed, eventually reassured; the household came back onto an even keel. Clara often spoke in after years of Brahms's help and kindness at this, the most appalling and most critical period of her entire life. He was a composer of genius, just making his way in the world; yet he laid all else aside in order to sustain his friends when without him they might have collapsed and the family disintegrated. And so Johannes Brahms acquired virtually paternal duties almost before he reached official man's estate. Beethoven had been obliged to accept duty as head of his family on the death of the mother; Brahms, at only a year or so older, had to assume at least temporarily a similar position in respect of another man's family. Again, it is a tribute to his integrity and firmness of character that he neither flinched from undertaking the duty nor failed in his execution of it.

Not that he would have wished to flinch or consider failure. His friendship with the Schumanns had already become one of the central experiences of his life: for Robert Schumann he felt a mixture of deep affection and true admiration; for Clara Schumann his feelings were immediately profound and complicated. But more than that, for the time being, was the effect upon his mind and sensitivity of the Schumanns' domestic fidelity and reciprocation. His own home life had been happy, but material circumstances had put a heavy strain upon it, not really helped by Jakob Brahms's habits of mild irresponsibility and fanciful optimisms; while Johannes's most direct experience of women had been of the disagreeable kind in the Hamburg *Lokale*. Now here before him was a fine, honourable, influential man and musician who had offered him friendship, and a paragon of a woman as his wife. No wonder Brahms, still a little unstable and unsure of himself in the company of the larger world, was more or less bowled over by both husband and wife.

It is beyond doubt that Brahms fell hopelessly in love with Clara Schumann almost from the outset. His earliest letters to her indicate the swift growth of an affection by no means solely platonic or filial; and all that followed afterwards but serves to emphasize that love and not friendship described the feelings of Johannes Brahms for Clara Schumann. There was no question here of disloyalty to Robert Schumann, or later to the memory of Robert Schumann; nothing of a conventional triangle, eternal or other. The relationship was complex, in essence more than complex, circumstances being what they were and Johannes Brahms being Johannes Brahms. Yet it cast a spell and an enmeshing net across the whole of his emotional life from now onwards, conditioned even when it did not determine virtually all else that went on inside him, behind the soon to be acquired armoured belt against which the world might fulminate as it would, and frequently did, without effect or possibility of penetration.

It was not a physically sexual relationship, ever, though it was inevitably a psychologically sexual one. Part of the key lies in Freud's theory of 'Degradation in Erotic Life', whereby sexual desire is so associated with bestial lust that where love exists desire cannot and where desire exists love is banished, something which is perfectly well understood today, but in the time of Brahms and Clara Schumann was not even hinted at in scientific research. Of course, it is by no means impossible that love and desire co-exist; indeed, that is the prerequisite for a balanced and successful relationship, the only kind that can or should endure. Yet where the 'degradation' syndrome operates the schism is often decisive and plummeting, for it will have in it the element of incest substitution, and it is hard to resist the belief that for Brahms to have slept with Clara Schumann would for him (and perhaps for her too) have been like sleeping with his mother. Freud argued that before we can free ourselves of the idea of sex as disgusting we have first to come to terms with the fact of incest, specifically with the idea of sex with mother and sister. Even today, when we think ourselves emancipated from old prejudices and taboos and imagine we have made some gesture upon the side of individual and social liberty, we have not yet accepted that contention in practice however much we may give it our theoretical approval in the privacy of our homes or upon some public platform from which we hope to win a reputation for 'progressive thinking', being intellectually 'with it', or whatever cant jargon happens to be in vogue at the moment. How much more decisive such psychological inhibitions must have been in the prudent, middle-class, bourgeois homes of the nineteenth century. The Wagnerian whole-hogging Romanticism might perhaps have encompassed such a proposition, and indeed the incest motif in *The Ring* is strong if partially concealed; but for Brahms and his like, there could have been no question.

Whether Brahms or Clara finally irrevocably decided that there should be no permanent union between them, because of the fourteen years' disparity in age, because of Clara's seven children, for any other practical (and therefore irrelevant) reason, is not clearly known and understood. It was probably never 'on' in any sense, despite what either or both may consciously have been tempted to think at one time or another. Deep gratitude and great womanly affection Clara felt for Brahms all the long days of their joint lives. For Clara, Brahms at first felt a darkly pure passion, part romantic young-in-heart, partly mother-figure orientated, and as the years grew and the shadows lengthened a human, indestructible, shored-up warmth of everlasting affection. How long it was that either, or again both, entertained some idea of a different outcome for them we can hardly guess at, for the most secret places of the human heart are closed, even against the ravishings and rapine of intent biography and lustful curiosities. Certainly there was at least one break on Brahms's side, as when in 1858 he became strongly attracted to a young singer, Agathe von Siebold, daughter of a university professor at Göttingen where Johannes had gone on his summer holiday. But Clara was there too—so was Brahms's young friend Julius Grimm from the Leipzig and Hanover days—and although Brahms was in love with Agathe for a year or so, it came to nothing. Brahms wriggled out, not at all admirably, and managed to offend both Agathe and Clara.

His excuse that he couldn't think of marrying while he was still not established and successful, and thus could not bear to face a wife's sympathy, simply will not wash. Even by Brahms's tactics of evasion it is a paltry thing.

In fact Agathe was always onto a loser. Clara's dominating, if unconscious (or was it entirely?) influence was upon everything. No doubt Brahms, a young man, sensitive, ardent, was spontaneously attracted to the pretty Agathe, also young, as he was capable of falling for other pretty women at various times in his life, though never so far as with Agathe Siebold. And no doubt there was some psychological relief in a turning of the affections away from the complex web of enmeshment with Clara Schumann, much senior, mother of many children, widow to be and then widow, to a 'normal' affair with an unencumbered charmer. But the deep pulls were too deep; the strong ties too strong. Brahms in the end, and afterwards, found ways to convince himself that singleness was the way for him; and when he once or twice seemed to be on the point of deciding, at least of wishing, otherwise, it was both too late and irrelevant. Now, with Agathe von Siebold, he backed down, ungraciously, saying that although he loved the lady, he could not bear fetters! With a lack of tact in keeping with his worst reputation, Johannes Brahms actually wrote those sentiments to Agathe herself. He cannot have been surprised that she took deep offence and did not forgive him wholly until she was old. What in essence he did was to hide from the complicated conscious-unconscious trap of his feelings for Clara behind the simple arithmetic of his worldly and material situation in respect of Agathe. He may have deceived himself: there is no reason why he should deceive us.

Brahms left a small memorial to his passing attachment for Agathe von Siebold in a theme embedded in the first movement of his G major string sextet, Op. 36, composed in 1864 and itself one of his most warm-hearted and romantically lyrical works. But even here Agathe won no victory: the first sextet, Op. 18, of 1860, was indelibly and absolutely Clara's. And so is most of the other music Brahms wrote thereabouts. But the two sextets are especially revealing. Simple division suggests a contrast between the B flat (classical) and the G major (romantic). Would it then be too much to hint that the 'pure' classical B flat enshrined his love for Clara while the more 'loaded' G major does the same for his brief feelings for Agathe? And then to mutter about sacred and profane love? It would be too much.

Yet a slight hesitation creeps into the mind in the presence of these two masterworks of Brahms's early manhood, each in its way so comprehensively *echt*-Brahms. He had worked at string quartets for some years; but nothing came of it or passed the strictness of his private censorship. It is said still that Brahms avoided publishing quartets for the same reason that he avoided symphony until he could virtually no longer avoid either, and for an obvious reason—in a word, Beethoven. But it is far more likely that in chamber music he began with quartets because that was the generally accepted medium of chamber music, and following the classical exemplars one would naturally and almost without thinking call upon four strings. But when you had taken thought, you may well have found that another combination or combinations suited you better and so you pulled yourself together and composed according to your natural lights and not by acquired habit. In the case of chamber music this was almost certainly the case with Brahms. He published three string quartets; but, although they contain fine music and are most skilfully wrought, hardly a man or woman I know will set them upon terms of equality in respect of pleasure given and experience received with the sextets, the string quintets, the piano quintet, the horn trio or most of all with the clarinet quintet. But the string sextet grouping was perfect for Brahms, with his strong penchant for instrumental polyphony and his predilection for dark colours.

But let us look more closely at these two sextets, often called by Brahms critics outstanding examples of his allegiance to classical forms and the classical style in music, against the solecisms and aberrations of the 'neo-German' heathens and self-styled progressives. Well, at some superficial and topline level, no doubt we have here a kind of modern (in 1860s reference) classicism. Yet underneath there is the firm, irresistible, romantic spirit moving. There is nothing peculiar in that; the romantic spirit often moves in Mozart, also in Haydn, most of the time in Beethoven. What is significant in these works of Brahms, and in many if not most to come, is the way in which the romantic spirit modifies and flexes the forms, largely through the movement of an adapted species of counterpoint. Even here, though, is not the nub of the matter. The B flat in particular is not noticeably polyphonic, though the textures are closely woven. The nearest reference is to Schubert; but the cast of mind and style are not at all Schubertian, and nor is the voice leading. Yet there is a certain blithe spirit in much of this Brahmsian music which may relate, because of its specific lyric impulses, to Schubert rather than to Haydn or Beethoven, to the Schubert of the C major string quintet most nearly. Perhaps Brahms never in all his life wrote so perfectly inspired a masterpiece as the Schubert quintet; but the lead and unconscious linkages are clear. The G major sextet, on the other hand, is richly polyphonic and pure Brahms end to end: a rich romantic hue over all. The slow movement variations of the B flat, though, contain one section, the third, with its 'storm music'—surging wildness underneath, sharp stabs and shafts of force above—purely and overtly romantic, and the following sweep of warm melody confirms the essentially Brahmsian cut and scope of the music, more than anywhere else echoing in its own orbit the anguished strife and lyric consolation of the D minor piano concerto.

The original form of the B major piano trio, Op. 8, is also indicative of Brahms's emotional turmoil at this time; a work full of youth's embattled ardour and idealistic vision. It belongs with the early piano sonatas rather than with the sextets, for it first appeared in 1854, which shows beyond doubt that the emotional turbulence was there all the time and not brought out exclusively by the tragedy of Robert Schumann, though, since it was begun in Düsseldorf in 1853 and completed in 1854, it almost certainly bears some witness to his conflicting feelings for Clara Schumann; and Niemann finds, 'hidden in this seething, shimmering finale of the first piano trio, with its deep stirring of emotion, the whole story of Brahms's love and suffering'.

Many years later, when Brahms was in his fiftieth year, he returned to this youthful trio and produced a completely revised version, the one that is usually heard today; and nothing is more revealing of the course Brahms's life took in its creative evolution than comparison between the two editions of the B major trio. No doubt the later version is more aesthetically satisfying; the original tends to long-windedness and lack of technical control. But there is a spontaneous freshness about it, the feel of absolute authenticity, and it is much to the credit of middle-aged Brahms that he did not lose all that made young Brahms so attractive, if immature.

What the later version really tells us is that Johannes Brahms, whatever else, did not die, and had no intention of dying, in the words of W. B. Yeats's fine poem *A Prayer for Old Age*, 'a foolish, passionate man'. He put all that behind him quite soon, as soon in fact as he had rationalized his passion for Clara Schumann and after the disaster of Robert Schumann's insanity and death had confirmed him in his view that nothing in life could be taken on trust.

But the decisive work here was the D minor piano concerto, which forever enshrines the immensity of the subjective agony raging inside him, the full magnitude of the internal conflict occasioned by his feelings for Clara and his torment over Schumann's breakdown, for the concerto is indivisibly linked to both, alike upon the external and the internal evidence.

The titanic opening of the D minor concerto, an undertaking that would have taxed the skill of the most experienced composer, is still often taken as indication of Brahms's 'immaturity', which caused him to ask of the forces he chose to employ more than they were capable of giving. In a sense perhaps it is true; but not in the way facile criticism would have us believe. The commonplace idea is that strings alone, tenuously supported by lower woodwind, are not strong enough to carry through that tempestuous opening, and horns at least are required to fill out the middle. And on paper the argument looks sound enough. But that leaves out of account precisely what Brahms was trying to express.

Looked at another way, that 'gapped' opening, agonized cries of violins above against a wild turmoil in the basses, with the menace of drums behind, may be seen as a most effective expression of Brahms's reactions both to the state of Schumann's mind when he flung himself into the Rhine and of his own confused and self-contradicting feelings for Clara with their bitter subconscious warring of idealistic young love and the incest-substitute bias of Clara as mother-figure. If, as has been long established by Kalbeck, this first movement of the D minor concerto was directly related to the desperate feelings of Brahms in the face of Schumann's attempted suicide, the whole work is no less clearly related to his love for Clara.

The second movement has in fact not a two-way but a three-way significance. On Joachim's score Brahms wrote over the slow movement the words: '*Benedictus qui venit in nomine Domini*'. Schumann was always known among his friends as '*Mynheer Domini*', so the words must be taken as indicating a direct tribute to Schumann. Yet Schumann himself had hailed the young Brahms as 'he that should come', so that there is also reference by implication that Brahms was accepting the mantle laid down by the dying Schumann. But Brahms wrote in a letter to Clara in December 1856, 'I am also painting a lovely portrait of you—it is the Adagio.' Thus the slow movement of the D minor concerto has a threefold aspect—Schumann, Brahms himself, Clara. There are of course counter-arguments to all these interpretations, though it is difficult to follow Geiringer's view that the Adagio is not at all in keeping with Schumann's character and therefore cannot be taken as referring to him, for much of it in lyric and melodic warmth and songful reflectiveness seems obviously Schumannesque. And since Schumann and Clara were so devoted and mutually sympathetic a couple, that the Adagio should refer to both seems entirely reasonable. It is true that Brahms subsequently struck the words out of Joachim's score; but this does not mean anything except that he decided after all not to make a public revelation of his musical intent: it does not alter the fact of it.

Even the final rondo with its echoes of a gipsy band, thought by many to be irrelevant in such a context, can be seen as bearing upon the overall reference of the concerto, for Brahms learnt from Reményi to love the gipsy music, and it had been at Reményi's instigation that he had set out upon the concert tour that led him eventually to the Schumanns' home in Düsseldorf. Thus the

Schumanns, Robert and Clara, must be seen as the central figures of the D minor concerto as it finally emerged, as they were the central experience of Brahms's early experience and were to remain so, one way and another, for the whole of the rest of his days.

The struggles the concerto had to find its ultimate form are themselves indicative of the relentless way it was hacked out of its composer through long hours of trial and torment. As is well known, it began as a sonata for two pianos; but Brahms was not satisfied, declaring that 'two pianos are not really enough for me'. Then he tried turning it into a symphony; but that did not pass muster either. Only by combining his own instrument, the piano, with the full resources of the orchestra could Brahms give apt expression to the fires and torments within him.

Even when he had finished the work, his tribulations were not over. The first performance under Joachim at Hanover was moderately well received; but the next, at the Leipzig *Gewandhaus* five days later, was a nerve-shattering failure of the kind Brahms had never experienced before and was never to be obliged to face again; something that would have thrown a less robust character into black pits of despair. Part of the trouble lay with the warring factions in Leipzig; with the 'conservatives' who considered Brahms a dangerous revolutionary and the 'progressives' who thought him a deserter from the cause of the 'new music'. These hissed and booed and derided, though probably as much to score points off each other as to put Brahms himself in his place. In between, the uncommitted Leipzigers found the work not at all what they were accustomed to in a concerto, having nothing of the virtuoso glitter and brilliance they expected in such compositions.

Though he took the failure with his customary philosophic calm and fortitude, it must have cut deep. And maybe it was in the Leipzig experience that he found reason to persuade himself, if no one else, when he had disentangled his association with Agathe von Siebold, that after failure he could not bear the consolations of a wife. And he was too honest with himself to blame the Leipzig audience entirely. He knew that the D minor in its first form contained flaws in its construction and certain miscalculations in its execution. These he resolutely set himself to correct, with the remarkably equable conclusion for one so young that a failure of this kind was 'the best thing that could happen to anyone'. He was unmoved in his conviction that the concerto would please one day; and though the critical acid is still at times applied to it, he has been proved right in his conviction.

Yet the D minor concerto does reveal immaturities and errors that no amount of revision at that time could eradicate. Some of the piano writing is clumsy: it is not so much that it lacks lucidity, for especially in the tormented first movement, preoccupied as it is with Schumann's mental breakdown and his own psychological complexes over Clara, lucidity is not what Brahms was after or what is required; but an occasional failure to make the interactive business of piano and orchestra properly effective. And the scoring is sometimes muddled in a way that suggests lack of orchestral experience rather than deliberate chaos designed to express mental and psychological instability from two different standpoints. But above all that, the D minor concerto is a direct and authentic transcript of Brahms's deepest and most tortured experiences at the time of its production. It also marks the end of Brahms's youthful romantic period. Never again was he to let himself go with such uninhibited passion; never again to wear his heart so unashamedly on his sleeve; never to let his guard so down that all the turbulence of his heart and mind would appear in his music, or in his life. Never again was he to seek an open battle with life through his public art on terms of exposed blood, sweat and tears. Not even in the C minor symphony, which strives heroically and publicly faces a number of major issues, but always from a position of considered vantage, the ship of life and art, as it were, fought from a heavily armoured and virtually impenetrable conning tower.

It would not be true to say that after the D minor concerto and the overwhelming experiences that in time's fruitful generation produced it, Brahms retreated from life. Those experiences themselves were in fact the culmination of much that had gone before, beginning with the facing of the harsh realities at their most unregenerate in the Hamburg *Lokale*. But the impact of Schumann's personal tragedy plus his own forlorn love for Clara with its 'forbidden' areas, concerned both with the incest-complex and the sense of unbreakable loyalty to the dead Schumann on both sides, was to reverberate throughout Brahms's subsequent life. It shudders through a number of compositions, some published long afterwards but conceived in the desperate mind at the time, to be distilled in the creative imagination into artworks coming to fulfilment only years later, like the C minor symphony and the piano quartet in the same key. But he did henceforth turn his back finally upon all extravagance and only allow as much of his inner life to appear on the surface as he quite consciously and deliberately wished to appear. If the openly passionate and impetuous side of his nature ever had the chance of taking command of him, its last full fling was in the D minor concerto.

But it never really did have the chance. In all that he wrote, early or late, there is ample evidence that he always intended to keep unbridled passion in its place. Even in the concerto where, if he wrings his own and our heart or threatens us both with the scent of subjective Armageddon, he quickly brings reassurance of quiet lyric song. If he elsewhere carries us towards the dizzier heights, he leads us not upon some reckless adventure but guides us with considered circumspection along the stoniest of paths, ropes secured firmly behind him. Whether it would have been otherwise had it not been for the twin happening of Schumann's tragedy and his love for Clara can hardly be guessed at. Much in his record suggests that he would have developed in the same manner as in fact he did even without those ineradicable experiences. Although the bias might have been different under different early personal and environmental experiences, it would have been only in degree, not in kind. Nothing would have turned him into a Wagner, or a Liszt, or anyone else. It was his necessity and his distinction as a creative artist that he should under every possible circumstance be himself. He was Johannes Brahms and no other, from the moment of his first appearance on this earth.

But one thing is certain, and can never be denied. Robert Schumann, to whose house he went as a young and still little-known provincial musician, unsure of his way yet sure in the knowledge that there was a way ahead for him, exerted the most powerful, formative and decisive influence on Brahms's personal and artistic evolution; on the first hand through his wife, and on the second through his example, his generosity and his publicly declared encouragement. It had by this time already become the central motif of his life; and it would recur constantly to the end.

When he knocked upon that door in Düsseldorf near the end of his wonderful year of 1853, all for him was to be changed— changed utterly.

5 A Living Reproach

'He was a living reproach to the haste of a superficial generation,'
James Huneker wrote in 1899, two years after Brahms's death.
'Whatever he wrought he wrought in bronze and for time, not for
the hour.' [1] If Huneker had been living and writing today, he
would have used words hardly less forceful, certainly no less
relevant to his own conception. He had, of course, his precedent;
and from no less a hand than Robert Schumann's, from the Preface
to the composer's *Collected Writings*:

> The state of music in Germany at that time [1833] can hardly be
> said to have offered any grounds for rejoicing. Rossini still reigned
> supreme in the theatre; among pianists, Herz and Hünten had the
> field pretty well to themselves. And yet only a few years had passed
> since Beethoven, Carl Maria von Weber and Schubert had lived
> among us! Mendelssohn's star was, to be sure, in the ascendant,

[1] p. 5.

and wonderful things were spoken of a Pole named Chopin; but their enduring influence would not be established for some years to come.[1]

Thus twenty years before Brahms knocked upon his door, Schumann discerned the hollowness in German musical life; and what is more, he set out to alter it. By the time Brahms arrived, Schumann's critical work was largely done; but the state of musical grace had still not, according to his lights, fallen upon the German nation. And since for Schumann, much more than for Brahms subsequently, the good and gracious had to be equated with what was German, he having a poor opinion of things Italian and a worse one of things French (making a partial exception for the case of Hector Berlioz), as soon as he saw a true genius of true German music, founded in the honoured traditions, sanctified by holy masters, he had no hesitation in playing John the Baptist to the new messiah. To his view the state of music in Germany had not much improved in those twenty years, despite his own efforts at correction and elucidation.

It is said that Schumann's extravagant championship of the young Brahms did more harm than simply put a heavy load upon immature and inexperienced shoulders; that he in fact set Brahms off upon a false trail and a barren path when he urged Johannes to lower his wand over the magic forces of chorus and orchestra; but that I do not believe. Brahms was destined from the beginning to grapple with musical composition on the largest, most demanding, scale. Though he loved and cherished in his secret heart the intimate beauties of lyric song and poem for keyboard, his cast of intellect and his vision into musical structure and architecture must anyway have led him to conquer symphony, concerto, commanding music for voices. The size and scope of the early piano sonatas tells us that, for they were composed when he had no thought but to make music his own way, no axe of any kind to sharpen and no hostile head to test it on.

Perhaps these and their like do show that he was mature before his time; that there was always an old head upon young shoulders;

[1] p. 13.

that what musical (or other) oats he may once have sown or hoped to sow were never all that wild. Though he had his youth and it revealed its passions, there was always underneath the restraining hand, conscious or unconscious: a severity of counterpoint and a turning of the back upon foolishness and excess, the stone concealing no unleashed serpent of indulged temptation.

How much, again, this was due directly to the Schumann tragedy, which must have sobered his already temperate nature still further, is hard to say. It meant, immediately, that he became virtual male head of the Schumann family, of his own act and volition, not in the sense of assuming the status of provider and winner of bread, but rather the reverse, of staying home while Clara went upon concert tours in order to sustain the family's material fortunes. A curious situation, and in the way it was as a duty taken up and discharged, both typical Brahms and nontypical Brahms—the first in the way he had ever that strong sense of moral responsibility towards life and art alike, and would shirk nothing that his conscience required; the second because he had always a fierce independence and would not allow himself to be sidetracked from what he had set out to do, and the absolute demands of the highest art to which he had dedicated his life, and responsibility for which Robert Schumann had passed on to him.

Thus there may at first seem a contradiction; a kind of dichotomy in his actions which must have been at odds. But if it is so, there can be but one explanation, or rather one catalyst: love; love for Clara herself principally, and through her for her children. In the light of his feelings for Clara Schumann, all would for him have fallen easily into place, his personal and human loyalty to her and to the memory of Robert Schumann, and his unflinching loyalty to the canons of giant art. And because both these loyalties were directly related to Robert Schumann, there would after all have been no real cause for damaging conflict or undermining dichotomy.

For two years, while Schumann still lived, his condition declining remorselessly and irreversibly while giving occasional signs of hope, were for Brahms's art and life both difficult and ambivalent. He continued to compose, and published a little; but he appears not to have made strenuous efforts to advance his own career. He introduced no major new works, though he appeared as pianist at several important concerts. Feeling that he had still much to learn, despite the unmistakable evidence he had already brought forward of his exceptional gifts for creation, he began during these years a self-imposed course of rigorous study, centring upon Bach, especially Bach's chorale settings and *Art of Fugue*. What he did compose and allowed to see light of day was often in the nature of study-work, like the piano variations, Op. 9 and Op. 21 (two sets). Though in all his production there is strong musical interest and that enduring quality with which all his compositions are indelibly stamped, it is clear that he was working his way towards greater things, notably to the great sets of variations on themes by Handel and Paganini, where the full force of his powers in variation writing is decisively exposed.

Although he played quite often in public, Brahms was never cut out for the role of virtuoso pianist. He both lacked the power of forceful self-projection and was fundamentally without the keenest desire to place an audience under that kind of spell, being more concerned with mastery of musical form and technique at its most profound. Composers have sometimes been also great executants; but taken in the round, the creative and the re-creative gifts do not walk easily hand in hand—which is why great conductors, pianists, violinists seldom succeed as composers, though their passionate desire often runs in that direction. Also Brahms's style of piano playing was not in accord with the public taste of the times. Audiences in those days required a coloured brilliance of execution, glittering scales and passage work, a surface of multifarious vividness, and were inclined to show shortness of temper if they didn't get it.

Taking the popular taste as it was and setting it beside Florence May's 'Personal Recollections' of Brahms, it is not at all difficult to understand why Brahms as pianist neither pleased his audiences overwhelmingly nor delighted himself beyond measure. As a youth he was too diffident to be a deliberate ear-catcher, and as he grew older his strong individuality of style and manner made him an excellent interpreter of his own music, but a reluctant one of other people's. In this respect he was the opposite of Joachim, a magnificent violinist and a gifted but largely superficial composer. This is not to call Joachim's profound musicianship into question: he was far from the empty-headed fiddler cutting out a profitable line with a handful of favourite works, but a true interpreter of original stature and the leader of one of the great string quartets.

The opposing biases of Brahms and Joachim worked to the considerable advantage of both during their long years of friendship and co-operation. In these 'Schumann' years of Brahms's life, he and Joachim began, at Brahms's instigation and urgency, a course of mutual studies in counterpoint, exchanging exercises with as much regularity as the more easy-going Joachim could sustain. Brahms rightly held Joachim's musical knowledge and culture in much esteem, and that he should have taken the violinist as his confidant during these crucial years is evidence of his perception as well as of his humility and sense of responsibility, for he had already made a bid for fame and won the plaudits of the musical world, yet he was now ready to see that as but a small preliminary to the main and most demanding part of his life.

Brahms's near sabbatical during these and the next few years may well have been occasioned by the disturbed nature of his emotional life as well as by his integrity and his unshakable determination to do full honour to his art. The whole Schumann business certainly brought on a major crisis in Brahms's life, and the internal evidence suggests that, long term, it was an artistic as well as an emotional and spiritual crisis. The resolution was long and the road to it hard, if there ever was a full resolution. The Schumann tragedy-and-love impact on Brahms was less a thing in itself than a culmination of all that had gone before; the hand of fate drawing its line from early poverty and frustration, from the nights in the Hamburg *Lokale*, through the emergence via Eduard Reményi and the first concert tour, the meeting with Joachim, and Liszt, to the welcome at Düsseldorf. Beginning in circumstances anything but auspicious and promising, Brahms's star rose quickly into the ascendant, only to come spiralling down again. No wonder if after that Brahms's innate caution and undeceived North German prudence finally asserted themselves and dictated the course of his subsequent life. When he reached Düsseldorf and Robert Schumann it might have jumped either way: though it was always likely to come down on the side of caution and prudence, had things gone otherwise and he had not been inescapably embroiled in Robert Schumann's breakdown and death and Clara Schumann's womanhood, a Brahms might have emerged which would not have been another and totally different Brahms, but one with a different blend and psychological balance. You cannot throw the dice against destiny, predict with accuracy how another turn might have come up, a different hand played. Yet the question is there to be asked.

At this time the whole of Brahms was coming into the open; all the facets of his creative personality emerging and beginning to fuse. Alongside the formal preoccupations of the variations and the passing off of the formal-cum-expressive problems of sonata for piano, that other intimate and lyric side of him was evolving on its own also. He had already composed and published songs, in collections issued as his Op. 3, Op. 6 and Op. 7, and here too he was launched upon a road that for him was always to be a main highway, one which led directly and inescapably to his personal hall of fame. Indeed, song was central to Brahms's nature as it was central to his compositions, one half of the total picture of his genius, one pole of his creative force; and many would say the most important half. But at this juncture in his developing career, it was instrumental evolution that appears to be the most important and formative; and in instrumental music the four Ballades, Op. 10, of 1854, thrust strong parallel lines into the future.

It has been said that in the Ballades Brahms was deliberately seeking more spontaneous and less formal means of working out musical material. This is unlikely: Brahms had already shown beyond much doubt that sonata and variations were not for him imposed formulae but his own natural way of thinking and feeling in music, the lyric element and romantic impulse already established as integral to both, for him. To say that Brahms deliberately turned from the larger forms to the smaller as the way out of a creative dilemma is the same as arguing that Schumann set him onto a false trail in the exhortation to tackle large-scale orchestral and choral composition. The constructional and the lyric were both essential ingredients of Brahms's creative faculty, indivisible facets of it, the opposition as well as the interaction between the two the indisputable fact of his genius, and to exalt one excessively above the other is to distort as it is to undermine the entire fabric of his musical creativity.

Precise definition of the nature of his two-way bias is, however, required if criticism is not to degenerate into vague generalizations and vapid speculation. The Ballades point a major direction—that of the old folk-poetry and legend, and the medieval character of the four pieces. This is something deep-sunk in Brahms, ranging right through to the slow movement of the Fourth symphony and some of the late piano pieces, notably Op. 117; the bardic element, heroic or lyrical. A number of works, vocal and instrumental, confirm this predeliction of Brahms, including the Four Songs for Female Voices, 2 Horns, and Harp, in which the best number is the last, *Song of Fingal*, a fine dirge based upon Ossian, the Ballades and Romances, Op. 75, which like the first of the piano Ballades of 1854 refers to Herder's version of the old Scottish ballad *Edward*, and much else. The medieval bias is no less strong and to some extent a corollary: *Marienlieder*, Op. 22, 'Magelone' Romances, many piano pieces, early and late.

Love of the Middle Ages was of course a typical Romantic attraction, often for intellectually untenable reasons, the delusion of the unclouded beauties of craft labour and the guilds set against the ugliness and inhumanity of the rapidly growing and engulfing industrialism. But the emotional response was both more certain and less corrupted. There is indeed something of a William Morris socialism about a certain species of Brahms composition, the *Marienlieder*, charming *a cappella* settings of traditional folk-poems relating to the Virgin Mary for 4-part mixed choir. These enchantingly innocent songs show Brahms's love and understanding of the old sixteenth-century German choral music as well as his immersion in German folk-lore. German too is the way in which these songs and some other Brahms music like them split a cunning difference between the Catholic and the Protestant religious outlooks—typically German because Germany was the one sizable country in Europe not finally given over to either Catholicism or Protestantism at the end of the religious wars of the seventeenth century and the Reformation and Counter Reformation. The Treaty of Westphalia had this effect also upon Germany, a religious as well as a secular division and fragmentation. This left its mark upon the growth of German music, and since Brahms was in the nineteenth century the most comprehensively German of all composers, its strong mark is upon him and what he wrote.

The Ballades, Op. 10, were once taken as being in essence the four different parts of one work adding up to a loose-framed sonata. The idea never had much to be said for it, and no doubt arose from the time when Brahms was promoted as the upholder of classical righteousness against romantic immorality and licentiousness and so everything he composed was as near as possible placed upon the classical counter, sonata form sought for everywhere. But in fact the Ballades, far from being parts of a sketched piano sonata, represent four differing aspects of Brahms's creative power away from sonata and variations form.

The first Ballade with its superscription from Herder's *Edward* leaves and can leave no doubt in the mind as to its intention and provenance: it might in the hands of Liszt have served for the opening of a sonata; but if it had it would not have been the same at all, and the continuation would have gone extensively elsewhere. For Brahms thus to begin a sonata work is wrong from the start. The second Ballade from another viewpoint looks into Brahms's future and end, for it suggests in its tone of quiet resignation those late piano pieces he called 'the cradle songs of my sadness', and although the tight concentration and formal dovetailing of those late pieces are not quite here, it is hard to resist the idea that already Brahms was unconsciously looking across the span of years to the inevitable sadness of his autumnal glow. The third Ballade again points a direction and once more stamps the name of Brahms upon the page of history, for it is the first instance of his use of the term *Intermezzo*, putting him thus into the bracket with Schumann but indelibly marking the piece with his own signature and no other.

Additionally, there is in the outlying parts of this number a touch, and more than a touch, of Frederic Chopin, in pianistic colouration and figuration, though again it is the particularly Brahmsian stamp of the music that enters the mind and remains there beyond all noticings and speculations upon the surface. Nor is what recollection of Chopin there is in any sense a matter of plagiarism, or copying, but of the sensitivity of a responsive artist to the general current and flow, the thought and feeling, of music overall in the time of his own ripening. The fourth Ballade is in the nature of an instrumental song, a simple folk-song couched in terms of solo piano with Brahms's particular and inimitable touch.

Thus the Ballades, though the least ambitious (or pretentious you may choose to say if you are not sympathetic to young Brahms) and in some ways the least aesthetically successful of Brahms's earliest compositions, are in a special way and manner pathfinders into the future, perhaps more than the sonatas since these had massive precedents and exemplars, for though originality and novelty are not in themselves virtues, here Brahms was breaking ground in an original way and forging links between the deeper strata of German popular life in poetry and music that were both characteristic of the age and profoundly significant for the contemporary consciousness.

The Ballades are also symptomatic of Brahms's clamping down and cooling off of his more unbridled romantic passions; transmuting the impetuous romanticism that shakes the formal rigidities of the sonatas into that reflective melancholy which was to become one of his most typical and penetrating ways of utterance. They stand in all ways in strong contrast to the resounding force of the sonatas and to the agonized excesses of the D minor piano concerto's first and most potent movement. Yet the matter of the Ballades was also in the sonatas: Brahms was not one to write some music exclusively out of one side or aspect of himself but other music from another and unrelated, as it might appear, side and aspect of himself. The slow movements of the sonatas, and quintessentially the 'Rückblick' of the F minor, related directly to the vein of lyric poetry and romantic impulse rooted deep in the consciousness which made the evolution of Brahms take the way and pace it did, and eventually had to.

One aspect of the sonatas, however, went with his youth and was never to return. That is the theatrical and externally spectacular element, which appears in much of the quick music but nowhere more than in the vaulted opening of the F minor sonata. It is asked why Brahms did not compose an opera and there has been speculation on what it would have been like if he had composed one. Both questions were certainly asked with fervour during his own lifetime, and if he provided no significant answer to either that was because he would never give answers, whether implicit or explicit, to any questions he wished to keep as his own business.

There is certainly evidence that he looked at times for a libretto, read some tracts and poems with that end in view; certainly he admired Verdi, adored Mozart's operas ever since the day when right at the beginning he and Lischen Giesemann had been taken to the opera in Hamburg to hear *The Marriage of Figaro* and had been so enchanted that both had cried aloud in delight; and for Wagner, despite the idiocy of the warring factions, he himself had respect and admiration. Yet upon every count it is clear that opera was not for him, certainly in no sense because he lacked the technical aptitude or constructive ability to maintain the kind of music he wrote over a long span, but because the texture and internal motion of his personality were not in that direction, after the D minor concerto had been wrung from him and he had looked deep into himself and taken the path indicated by the Ballades rather than the hugely propulsive and instinctively dramatic sonatas. The theatrical went from Brahms with the passionate outpourings of his youth: thereafter he cultivated the contemplative rather than the overtly dramatic, reflective introversion rather than coloured extroversion. This was the temperament rather than the deliberate choice of Johannes Brahms.

A look at Brahms's mature music that has, or might have had, a dramatic-operatic background but confirms this indisputably. *Rinaldo*, for example, the 'cantata' for tenor, male voice chorus and orchestra that is often supposed to have been Brahms's nearest approach to the operatic style. Despite some superficial appearances, a tilt or so there, a gesture here, *Rinaldo* is fundamentally no nearer to opera than the *Rhapsody*, also to words by

Goethe, and few things can be less operatic than that. *Rinaldo* is illuminating from several points of view. The subject matter, from Tasso in a poem composed by Goethe specifically for setting to music, concerns the deliverance of the crusader knight Rinaldo from the wiles and allurements of the temptress Armida, the story itself familiar enough from classical literature and even relating back to the Odysseus and Circe fable; and the idea is almost a cliché of romanticism, much explored especially by Richard Wagner both early and late, in the Tannhäuser-Venus and the Parsifal-Kundry involvements. The basis of holy innocent and wicked temptress is probably naïve in any case and tends to weaken all art works in which it directly appears (it is no surprise that the second Act of *Parsifal* is the really impossible one to take seriously, despite Wagner's immense genius and inexhaustibly resourceful cunning).

Yet in all this one has the decided impression that for Wagner and the Romantics the pursuit of Kundry-Venus indulgences is not quite the terrible sin it may be presented as and that liberation therefrom is often imposed rather than ardently desired and that redemption is not achieved without regretful backward glances. Though the motif of redemption through the love of a good woman and Divine dispensation was strongly entrenched in the Romantic attitude, one way or another, there is always the strong contrary pull, the delights of abandonment to sensual pleasure deep-rooted in the human psyche and forsworn only with reluctance.

But for Brahms it was always different. There was no contrary pull; and it is clear that the appeal of the *Rinaldo* poem was primarily ethical, the victory over seductive temptations through manly self-control to be sought for its own sake and without ultimate reward. Thus Brahms's music reflects accurately his own rugged North German rectitude, has the tone of sturdy bourgeois morality and is nowhere rippled by sensuous diversions. In Goethe's poem, and so in Brahms's cantata, the sorceress Armida does not appear in person; her wiles and seductions are invoked only by description and, in a sense, by implication. The poem is not in itself dramatically effective, so perhaps it is not entirely fair to judge Brahms's ability to write theatrically potent music on its evidence alone. On the other hand, nothing that he wrote in any form suggests that his creative faculty worked easily in such terms. True, until quite late in life he interested himself in the possibility of composing opera, and appeared willing to consider libretti. In 1870 he told Clara Schumann that Wagner's work would not deter him from undertaking such a project; and it seems to have been as late as 1888 that he finally decided not to trouble his mind further with it, declaring to his friend Widmann, himself a librettist who had long sought to bring Brahms's operatic ambitions to a head, that he had resolved 'to try neither an opera again—nor marriage'. Widmann had tried in vain to interest Brahms in libretti based upon a play or a Calderon translation by Gozzi; but although a seed may have been planted, it was destined never to grow and produce issue.

Brahms and opera is at the first sight an intriguing question; but it ceases to be worth bothering with once the true nature of Brahms's temperament and creative nature is fully understood. Here again Hans Gal lays a false trail. Gal says that 'it is useless to speculate on what the style of a Brahms opera would have been', on the same basis that it would be impossible to imagine a Beethoven opera if Beethoven had not written one. But it is quite easy to predict the course of a Beethoven opera even without *Fidelio :* you have only to understand Beethoven and then make the correct deductions in order to arrive at a pretty clear idea of *Fidelio*. Beethoven's temperament was essentially dramatic; his use of sonata form in symphony, concerto, piano sonata, string quartet is dramatic in all its aspects. But although there is drama of a kind in Brahms's orchestral and instrumental music, it is never of the Beethoven kind, either technically or psychologically. Key relationships, rhythmic juxtapositions, harmonic movement, in Beethoven all work, individually and collectively, in the direction of dramatic release, but in Brahms, despite the inattentive criticism which once tried to set him alongside Beethoven in the evolution of German music, the effect is not only dissimilar but usually diametrically opposite. It is not a question of moral or ethical bias: both Beethoven and Brahms are essentially 'moral' composers. But with Beethoven the interaction of the constituent elements of composition lead to resolution through dramatic clash, with Brahms they lead more naturally to the philosophical contemplation of moral issues.

Beethoven too sought long for another libretto, upon which he might base a successor to *Fidelio*. Various subjects were suggested to him, and some caused a momentary crisis of excitement. But in the end none implanted the true and fertile seed in his creative compost. For Beethoven sonata form as he himself used and exploited it was the true stuff of drama. He learned that lesson with the overtures to *Fidelio*, and with other dramatic pieces like the *Egmont* and *Coriolan* overtures, the dramatic essence concentrated into the orchestral prelude with the compressed organic power of almost nuclear force. Thus for Beethoven the appeal of drama was innate and inescapable, though he responded to it in his own way, which was not fundamentally, and despite *Fidelio*, the way of the theatre. But for Brahms the clash of opposing forces moved less in the direction of straight dramatic confrontation than in that of philosophical interaction, of 'if and precisely and but' as one might choose to describe it. Not for Brahms the direct statement hurled in defiance or proposed as unequivocal thesis and antithesis, the dramatic collision driven home with impassioned urgency, the broad tonic and dominant swing carrying all before it as in Beethoven's middle period compositions, but the reflective mind's strong but usually undemonstrative speculation upon the complex matter in hand. A difference not in degree but in kind; the forms of music apparently similar at times but behind the appearance a creative faculty devoted to other ends by other means.

Rinaldo shows that Brahms knew his *Fidelio*, notably in the *scena* for tenor solo with oboe, the inference direct and unmistakable. But the effect is not at all *Fidelio*-like, either in tone or in psychological impact. Nor is it intended to be. With Brahms the matter in hand is considered, deliberated upon, mulled over, presented in music of firm consistency. But nowhere is it revealed in straight dramatic terms; exposed in the direct clash of personality or conflicting ideas. The true dramatic composer would have gone about it very differently, resorting to devices of theatrical action and motivation, throwing the salient points into forceful relief, colouring the whole with the emotional entanglements and opposing loyalties of the knight in a dilemma. Nothing of this in *Rinaldo*, and so I think that Brahms's search for an opera libretto was never all that serious, however much he may at various times have tried to convince himself, for it was an idea with which his mind toyed but did not spring from the deepest needs of his creative nature.

The successful opera composer should have a number of specific qualities, among them the capacity for self-dramatization and the power of histrionic gesture. Neither of these Brahms possessed. Not all who have them turn to opera, or to some form of dramatic production—Mahler, for instance. Mahler, music's inescapable self-dramatist and master of the histrionic gesture, wrote no opera. For Mahler, symphony with or without voices was sufficient, as in a totally different sense it was for Beethoven, whom none would see in those terms. Yet Beethoven had his huge power of self-projection and self-dramatization, and his gift of gesture if not exactly histrionic was intensely dramatic also. But Beethoven had the ability of transcendence of the self in the narrow and inhibiting sense, the hard-won capacity of escape from the inhibiting grip of the ego; and it was this force of the self combined with the transcendence of the self which led to the consummate art of the third period and sets him ultimately among the small handful of the world's supreme creative artists.

Brahms's path was a different and more humble one, as he himself well knew. Those who place or have sought to place him upon that same pinnacle do him a major disservice, for by setting him in that false position they considerably diminish his real stature. I think that Brahms's true position in music history is still obscured, and where it is not clear it is because he had too often been set upon a conjunct course with Beethoven. Brahms is nearly always at his best and most himself when he is furthest from his great predecessor. He himself was only too aware of that huge shadow looming behind him, and much as he revered Beethoven he once confessed that it was difficult to compose with such a giant breathing down his neck. Brahms-Beethoven, the 'three

Bs', and all nonsense of that sort but places the true image of Brahms under a distorting lens and at its worst has prevented any accurate conception at all of Brahms from emerging in either historical or aesthetic perspective. But if we say that Brahms's path was a humbler one than that of Beethoven, crossing the latter at no significant point, that is not to diminish Brahms's real stature and achievement, only to see him as he truly was and thus, on the contrary, to lift him to his real position, sure then in the knowledge that no argument or prejudice can remove him from it; for a man may often appear diminished when he is set beside one of obviously greater stature, yet come into his full force and magnitude when seen by his own true light and in his correct context. A man, as Jonathan Swift observed, may be a pygmy among giants but a giant among pygmies.

Yet in one sense there is an inescapable point of contact between Brahms and Beethoven: the one initiated and the other continued the strong and ineradicable moral tone in music in a frequently 'immoral' age. There is little true correspondence between the music of Beethoven and the music of Brahms; but the 'tone' of both shows unmistakable similarities. And it is here that Brahms may be said to justify Huneker's claim for him as a living reproach to the haste of a superficial generation, for despite all temptations and seductions, even if for him they were never as strong and insistent as for many of that romantically hued nineteenth century, Brahms never wavered from his profoundly moral artistic purpose. Whatever else may be said about Brahms, he was an artist of iron integrity, deeply aware of his responsibility both to his art and to the German nation in which he took such irreproachable pride.

That Brahms did not write an opera and in the end discerned that such a course was not for him, realizing perhaps down inside him that his ambitions towards opera were fundamentally spurious anyway, is indicative both of his true bias of temperament and of his subjective integrity. I am not going to say that opera is a frivolous art—Wagner alone would be sufficient answer to that idea in the nineteenth century, and Verdi would confirm it—but it is true that much operatic production has come from obviously third-rate composers and many successful and popular operas are musically barren, or worse, the poverty of the creative talent concealed behind stage 'business' and crudely blatant emotionalism.

When Francis Toye said that Puccini was not a great composer because he was not a great man, he exposed with ruthless precision the empty posturing of a great deal of operatic fare. We need not write off the sheer effectiveness, the unquestioned charm and appeal of Puccini's operas—and not only Puccini's, not only Italian operas but many German ones also—in order to see that such contrived artificialities would never have passed and been found acceptable away from the stage and its conventions. Brahms is often still accused of 'faking' when he finds himself stuck for bobbins and short of inspiration in large-scale works, and in places it is true. But nothing that Brahms ever did by way of giving short change and falling back upon the convenience of a convention to cover his tracks, is anything compared with the musical faking in melodramatic romantic operas. It must be remembered too that at this time Rossini was all the rage in the theatre, and to men of the cast of temperament of Schumann and Brahms, and also to Beethoven, Rossini was the height of frivolity and artifice, the living evidence of Italian frivolity compared with German seriousness and dedication. Beethoven himself had objected to certain of Mozart's operas because the subjects were frivolous, and when looking for suitable libretti the great Beethoven had made it perfectly clear that he was determined to avoid all such triflings.

No one would pretend that Mozart was not a great composer because he was not a great man: the idea is so preposterous that it will not easily lie upon the page at all, even to be dismissed. Nor does the 'frivolity' of the texts of certain Mozart operas like *Cosi fan tutte* indicate a lack of true seriousness on the part of the artist Mozart: indeed, such operas, including *The Marriage of Figaro*, to which Beethoven, music's incorruptible moralist, also took exception, are among the most treasured and treasurable products of Mozart's unique genius. All the same, it is not difficult to see why Beethoven, and after him Brahms, must have sought for opera libretti of a very different cut and cast; must have looked, that is, for subjects more in accord with their own highly moral and ethical temperaments. Thus Brahms was only ever likely to be attracted to subjects with a high moral tone, and even then would have been suspicious of what the entire venture might lead him into, his own mind being not of the kind willing to compromise with theatrical convention.

Rinaldo from this point of view does show how Brahms might have proceeded if he had allowed himself to be tempted into opera. He was essentially a 'Rinaldo-man', a staunch resister of temptations and seductions, keeping both resolutely at bay, firmly entrenched behind the diamond shield. Maybe too opera was a kind of temptation for Brahms in itself, and one that had ultimately to be resisted as by some inner force of unrevealed necessity.

In so far as Italy was for the Germans associated with ideas of Latin frivolity and laxity—though it was really France rather than Italy that excited their particular contempt, especially after the Franco-Prussian War had proved the superiority of holy German arms against the decadent French with Paris seen as the particular plague-spot—Brahms's relations with Italy are of illuminating interest. Brahms loved Italy dearly; he made frequent journeys there and revelled in the Italian graces of life and in the warmth of the sun upon his North German back. He always looked forward to his Italian trips with Widmann, and wrote warmly about them, both in retrospect and in anticipation of more to come. Italy always seems to have lifted his spirits and sharpened his perceptions. No doubt much of the impact was psychological. The *nouveau-riche* element in the German mentality, with its frequent aggressiveness and an overbearing attitude, led, predictably, to an underlying sense of insecurity, a concealed inferiority complex for which the aggressiveness was the familiar protective shield, so that Italy, as an historic centre of European civilization, exerted a strong psychological pull.

It has been said that the German sense of inferiority was the result of the cultural ascendancy of Austria, and of Vienna in particular, for so many centuries; and I think that is true. But Italy, in a different way, as the non-German core of civilization, also acted strongly on the German consciousness. No doubt Brahms, the proud German patriot, immediately aware of no shortcomings in German life and outlook, did not think of Italy

as superior in basic civilization, or go there for the conscious purpose of uplifting his view of life by direct contact with the best
Europe could offer. But it is likely that his subconscious did feel
itself liberated by the historical greatness of Italy in art and creative
genius, as well as by the sun, the warmth, the gaiety and grace of
the country. He was well versed in Italian history, had a good
knowledge and appreciation of Italian art and architecture as well
as of the old Italian music; and his astute intelligence no doubt
took in and acknowledged all that Italy stood for. Much that is
sunny and gracious in his own music came out of his Italian travels,
even if little in it shows a direct influence of Italian melody and
dramatic contrast.

Though he never learnt to speak good Italian and always preferred to travel with someone who did, Brahms loved Italy and the
Italians so much that his idea of both seems to have had a good
spicing of idealization in it. True to himself and to his humble
origins, he did not care to mix in Italian high society, but made his
way to ordinary hotels and restaurants, and kept his best company
with the common people. Even when he was famous and well off,
he did not alter his habits abroad, any more than he was prepared
to any great extent to alter them at home. And he seems to have
been a good traveller, tactful, full of respect for local ways and
customs, nothing at all like the all too familiar boorish German
tourist of yesteryear, forever throwing his weight about and causing unnecessary offence by vulgar displays of imagined superiority
—which is of course the classic defence against suppressed feelings
of inferiority. That the Germans often did behave like that can
hardly be disputed; and even today it is not unknown or unobserved. Goethe saw and understood this tendency long before
Brahms made his way into Italy, or anywhere else, for he once
remarked, sadly, to Eckermann, as he looked upon a crowd of
young Germans rowdily disporting themselves in the streets of
Weimar, that 'another two hundred years must pass before people
will say: "It is long since they were barbarians."' Maybe he
would have had cause to say that about Brahms at certain times,
for Brahms could be very boorish and uncouth in certain moods.
But there is no reason to suppose that Goethe would have felt the

need to censure Brahms for his behaviour abroad. Perhaps Italy had its civilizing, its engracing effect upon the peripatetic Johannes too.

But Brahms did not visit Italy until 1878, and he did not go with Widmann until ten years later. The first visit of all was not un-clouded sunshine and happiness, for during it he went to Palermo, where his god-child Felix Schumann was dying of consumption and desperately trying to prolong his frail years with the help of the Southern Italian sun. Whatever else Brahms went to Italy for, or what inner need drew him back there eight times, it was certainly not his health. His constitution was ever robust, and until he was well advanced in age he regularly outwalked and exhausted his companions wherever he and they chanced to be. But seeing poor Felix, last son of Robert and Clara Schumann, born at the time of Robert Schumann's final collapse and at the time of Brahms's most intimate involvement with the family, must have cost him a bitter tear. If so, he bore it with his usual fortitude; and it did not, and could not, do anything to dampen that rich love of Italy that was never to leave him after he had first come to it on this 1878 trip through the sun-laden south.

Yet if Brahms did not find Italy until 1878, his lifelong habit of taking creatively fruitful summer vacations was soon established. He spent various summers at Pörtschach in Carinthia, at Thun in Switzerland and at Ischl in the Salzkammergut in his later years. There were sojourns in other pleasant resorts too, and a number of tours abroad in the interests of music directly. For a largely sedentary and apparently unadventurous fellow, Brahms was a pretty insistent traveller. He liked seeing new places, and despite his reputation for boorishness and bad temper, he always enjoyed meeting and mixing with other people.

Perhaps it was some legacy of the cultural as well as the physical inhibition of his early years that encouraged him to be up and about in the outer world. Compared to Beethoven, he was positively restless; and compared to Bach he was almost a demon of vagrancy. And here too, I think, is a further misconception about him: the image of grumpy Brahms sitting austerely at home writing stodgy Teutonic music and virtually daring people to find it alluring or

plainly enjoyable, setting out from time to time to be rude to anyone unlucky enough to fall foul of him and then returning home
through shadowy streets to the lonely bed of the misanthrope and
misogynist. It will not do. Neither the beard nor the paunch of
later years can permanently obscure the real and true Johannes
Brahms, a man of warm heart and yearning soul, the composer of
music of no less warmth and yearning, even if in both respects
sometimes defeating his own ultimate end of at bottom wanting
to be loved. The shyness, awkwardness, sharp-tongued crust of the
man, all that has been and can be set against him or charged to his
account as a none too amiable person and artist is countered
effectively by what may be set upon the opposite side, though it
was occasionally hidden behind the taking-in façade. To call him
the living reproach is not to acquiesce in the old idea of the thick-
skinned recluse, a kind of rhinoceros composer, ever ready at the
charge, head and sensitivity as hard as the hide and no less cross-
grained.

And the travelling Brahms, full of both curiosity and goodwill,
is an essential part of the full picture, a light of sure revelation
contributing to the complete picture more complex than is often
supposed when naïve legend and old cliché are allowed idle per-
petuation. Travel, of course, was one of the Romantic avocations,
born in the late eighteenth-century habit of the Grand Tour but
other-orientated in the Romantic age, after Byron, Shelley, Liszt,
innumerable others, making the travel a form of escape from or
challenge to the inhibiting conventions of the social world upon
the one hand, or the subjective dramatic gesture upon the other,
and as often as not the two at the same time. Brahms, making
perhaps another small adjustment when his travelling was not
upon strict business, voyaging not as gesture or as blessed escape
but upon the sound principle of pure private pleasure, still revealed
much of himself *en voyage*, and because he was a true artist for
whom everything is grist to the creative mill it was reflected in his
music; indeed, more than reflected, it became an inescapable
ingredient beneath the surface of a number of his compositions.

There was nothing of Childe Harold about Brahms, upon the
immediate top plane; yet also because he was a true artist, the

restless, wandering element that is in all men, though it is often controlled and sometimes denied, came out as he made his way around the world, and most of all in the Italy he loved beyond simple enjoyment of sun and good cheer but as something that struck deep into the complementary essence of his human being and nature. No clearer evidence of this can be found, or is needed, than Widmann's 'Recollections', for from these we know not only what travels in Italy meant for Brahms but also exactly what manner of man emerged and was revealed upon those travels. It suggests, as I say, another small adjustment of the conventional, old-conjured idea of him.

In calling Brahms the 'living reproach' in Huneker's term we set him down still more securely as the representative in music of the nineteenth-century bourgeois age. Maybe today especially that will be a sure mark against him, the unquestioned limitation against which no counterforce can prevail, for we have come to a time when 'bourgeois' is a term of abuse in many minds, anathema to the young and everything they must rebel and protest against, representative of the old constricting world dying now of its moribund traditions and stiff with the rigidity of obstinate longevity. But it was not always so: the bourgeois age that perhaps came to an end, with so much else, in August 1914, had great achievements to its credit upon all planes, the technical and industrial, the political and social, the artistic; and the music of Johannes Brahms was among the most distinguished and enduring of those achievements. The Romantic element in Brahms was a bourgeois romanticism, unexaggerated, unostentatious, restrained, but running deep and firm, as also in Schumann; the morality in Brahms was the bourgeois morality lifted from the rut and enlivened from within by the power of creative genius, but occasionally over-formal, too rigidly conventionalized.

If the virtues of Brahms's music are far above any social or economic virtues, its faults are for the most part honest and homey bourgeois faults; not the wild and extravagant faults of aristocracy; not the mixed explosive and damped faults of the proletariat; but those precisely of the bourgeoisie as a class, though in fact the true bourgeois mind and mentality spreads through and beyond all barriers of class or social stratification, even if it is predominantly middle class in both origin and outlook.

If the eighteenth century was the culmination and perhaps apotheosis of the age of aristocracy, and the twentieth has been that of threat to a stabilized order by proletarian challenge, the nineteenth century was the age of the bourgeoisie, at least in the core and centre, and certainly in that new and powerful German Empire which Bismarck had created and of which Johannes Brahms was a chief adornment. Thus if one is wholly antipathetic to the bourgeois spirit and outlook, if one is resolutely set against all that the middle class in its forward movement has achieved and sought to achieve, blind to all but its errors of narrow conventionalism, spurious 'morality', regard for appearances in place of substance, one cannot really feel at one with the music of Brahms at its deepest, most potent, level. It is not in the end, though, a matter of political or social or economic fact, but of spiritual insight and emotional sympathy below a surface often encrusted with pretence and clouded by hypocrisy.

Yet what precisely is this bourgeois spirit of which Brahms was the foremost representative in music? It has many facets, is not to be summed up or dismissed in a word, for it spans a broad area of human experience from which few are entirely free without some loss of common humanity. Essentially, the bourgeois attitude and outlook express love of security based upon sure foundations, the continuity of traditions permitting at the same time considerable flexibility and the means of change without self-destruction, and an attachment to institution and establishment. These at their lowest can be cramping and inhibiting ideas, soon becoming enslavers; the idea of permanence moving towards the moribund, the idea of continuity stifling truly new and creative growth. But at the other end, at the highest level, they may have considerable liberating force.

Another bourgeois characteristic is the insistence upon the practical—the area where the characteristic bourgeois sentimentality is rooted, for none is more sentimental than the practical man for whom every action must have a defined and definable end in view, every thought lead to a 'productive' act. This too is set upon the debit side; but again must I say that all is not upon that debit side, and today, when nothing is taken for granted, held in traditional esteem or accorded unquestioning respect, re-definition of the bourgeois virtues as well as insistence upon bourgeois faults, after the conventional and facile 'revolutionary' habit of passing off attitudes for ideas and slogans for thoughts, is a major necessity of historical analysis. Certainly it is necessary when one approaches a composer like Brahms, indivisibly linked as he is to that bourgeois age and era.

The bourgeois idea is itself basically a romantic emanation, in contrast to the aristocratic idea, with its centrality of inheritance and therefore of individual limitation, which represents the classical ideal within the social framework. Opposition to the bourgeois idea is also frequently romantic in origin, the opposition to and protest against convention, establishment, tradition, in whatever form it may take, so that the bourgeois idea stands in a dual relationship to the force and current of romanticism, providing foundations both in the pro and in the contra sense. Thus in the bourgeois age of the nineteenth century, both Brahms and Schumann on the one hand, and Wagner and Liszt and Berlioz on the other, were directly related emotionally and intellectually to the bourgeois foundations. For Brahms, as for Schumann, though even more than for Schumann, the German bourgeois life was central to his life and experience, himself directly a product of it. And in the sense that the bourgeoisie was at that time the bulwark of the social and political structure of the age, not only in Germany but most strongly in Germany, so the bourgeois spirit is the bulwark and essential mainspring of Brahms's music.

Though such a statement may at certain times and in certain contexts seem paradoxical, and possibly inimical, it is necessary first to understand the truth in it before one can begin to contradict or basically modify. It is through-running, all-informing, casting its meaning upon every side. Patriotism may not be a particularly bourgeois sentiment; but it tends in that emotional and social environment to take on an identifiable character. And it was the character of Brahms's patriotism, strong, deep-flowing, romantic. The music it inspired thus has those same qualities of strength and romantic idealization. Again, if the bourgeois conception of patriotism is at bottom romantic and idealized, that associated with aristocracy is classical in its hierarchy and fealty of position as much as of person.

Of Brahms's overtly patriotic works, the most imposing, *Triumphlied*, Op. 55, was the culmination of a sequence of vocal compositions of the 1860s, a sequence so direct that the Op. numbers from 41 to 66 are virtually unbroken output of vocal music, solo or choral, interrupted only by the two string quartets in C minor and A minor (Op. 51), the St Antoni Variations (Op. 56) and the Third piano quartet (Op. 60 but the final solution of an earlier problem first sketched many years earlier). This remarkable sequence includes some of Brahms's greatest songs and choral music, including the *German Requiem* (Op. 45), the Alto Rhapsody (Op. 53), *Schicksalslied* (Op. 54) and the *Liebeslieder Walzer* (Op. 52), as well as many sets of songs containing some of his greatest individual numbers. Unlike Schumann, Brahms was not usually one to become obsessed with one genre or category at a time: his creative faculty functioned too integrally, too much as a unity, for that sort of self-division to be much in evidence. Yet this decade, more accurately from about 1864 to 1874, stands out for the range, quantity and quality of its vocal productions.

Triumphlied, though the most direct expression of Brahms's German patriotism, is neither jingoistic nor hysterically 'nationalist', but a form of massive self-satisfaction at the thought of just victory, of reflective contentment in unashamed pride of race and blood and nation. The tone is hardly political in any narrow or noisy sense, and it is not surprising that this composition, though highly honoured in Germany, even at one time set incongruously above the *Requiem*, has never, under Kaiser or Führer, been made an anthem of German militarism and breast-beating—something for which the shade of Johannes Brahms has no doubt somewhere expressed a quiet and caustic satisfaction, leaving to the real but not hated rival, Richard Wagner, the distaste and annoyance of being dragged into the modern political cesspit and made the prop of shame and dishonour. But it was inevitable, in Brahms's case anyway: Brahms's patriotism was never of the kind readily open to squalid exploitation, for it came from within as integral part of the total world- and life-view and was not imposed from without and paraded in enmity.

Triumphlied, for eight-part chorus and probably suggested initially by Handel's *Te Deum* for the Peace of Utrecht and Dettingen, was composed specifically to celebrate the victory of Prussian arms against the French in 1870–1, that resounding triumph of the modern rising German power over the traditional valour and homogeneity of the French, which led out of its conclusion to the realization of the pan-German ideal, the German 'idea' to which Bismarck had devoted so much labour and wily patience. Both in the history of modern Europe and in the life story of Johannes Brahms, those events were momentous. *Triumphlied* is in its way momentous too.

The centrality of vocal music in Brahms's catalogue, not only during a particular period, throws invaluable light upon his creative depth, most of all in its subtle relationship to the past and the pre-classical composers of vocal music, not only German but Flemish, French, Italian also. Brahms had an extraordinarily sensitive ear for the differences between various types of vocal writing, and his imaginative penetration of the styles and idioms of the past enabled him—compelled him more accurately—to make subtle internal adjustments in his own composition in differing contexts. The importance of this to the modern Brahms critical biographer is inestimable, for it shows not only the range and depth of his musical culture, acquired by his own effort rather than instilled by formal instruction, but also the fundamental bias of his creative gift. It bears upon his instrumental as well as upon his vocal music and informs his style at virtually every move, adding frequently a special flavour and colour not otherwise easy to track down. I am indebted to the American scholar and choir director Edward Tatnall Canby, whose Canby Singers contribute so valuably to American musical life and to the international record scene, for some frank and generous private correspondence on this subject. Edward Canby claims, though I only half believe it, not to have done 'systematic research at all into the "influence" matter—it has simply hit me in musical terms, as we have sung through a fair part of the Brahms *a cappella* music, which I dearly love for its immense singability, its honesty and, most of all, its marvellous sense of history and the past, brought into such perfect "harmony" with Brahms's own idiom'.

'My feeling [Canby continues] is simply that we today (some of us—quite a few relatively speaking) are now so familiar with the earlier musical literature, and in such a newly "authentic" form, that new analogies between Brahms and the old music come out almost automatically, whereas the older Brahms commentators, whose works are mostly still current and standard, simply did not really know this older music. Schütz, for instance, is now ultra-familiar to our young singing groups, including mine. Also many an older composer including, for instance, Isaak, who is widely known among our "Renaissance"-type groups; Gallus, LeJeune, Pierre de la Rue (to go into the French area), and many of the "Flemish" or Netherlands composers, notably Josquin, whose music we read straight off as familiarly as William Byrd out of England. We are, indeed, familiar with so many of these—back to Okeghem, Obrecht, Dufay, all of whom "go" very nicely in choral format—that to sing Brahms is to hear their ways of doing things the instant that there is even a suggestion of them. And there are many.

'Offhand, I would mention as examples, first and foremost the utterly easy writing of five- and six-part textures. Who else in the 19th century could do that? A striking facet. Then, in detail, such things as the uneven phrase lengths (except in folk-type music), the use of the ultra-familiar (in old music) "hemiola"—six beats divided into twos, against threes, in cadences; the often deliberately simple harmonies, very much as in older music; the skilful use of old modes—NOT as Holst and Vaughan Williams revived them out of English folk song but in a much more exact evocation of the earlier pre-18th century manner, common to *all* earlier music. (B. particularly loved the Phrygian mode, and used it as did Bach but with a more 17th-16th century feel than Bach's.) Then there is the whole matter of word setting—so perfectly modelled on such as Schütz, Schein et al.'

These remarks gain much in force and meaning because their author is a practical musician, director of a choir, as well as a profound musicologist, and so his observations are based upon and derive from immediate experience 'in the ring', as one might put it. Yet I incline to wonder if the former Brahms commentators were so unaware of the deep influence of the old music and so unfamiliar with that music itself as Edward Canby implies. No doubt actual performance of the composers he mentions and many others of a like line and lineage was rare in days before the second half of the twentieth century; and almost certainly, with but few exceptions (of whom Brahms himself appears to have been one of the foremost), the old music was misunderstood where it was known in the nineteenth century. All the same, the fact of Brahms's indebtedness was widely recognized.

Edwin Evans, in the volume devoted to Vocal Music in the indispensable *Handbook*, draws specific attention to Brahms's study and understanding of the music of Palestrina, and in various other places of the influence of medieval music; and Florence May, writing of the first performace of Brahms's *Ave Maria* and *Begräbnisgesang*, observes that the latter in particular 'gives evidence of the strong impression he had derived from his exhaustive study of the medieval church composers'. True, neither Florence May nor Edwin Evans, nor in fact most other earlier Brahms critics, indicate that they have practical experience of the old medieval music, and none of the names listed by Edward Canby, and considerably added to upon other occasions, appears in their books' indexes or texts. But it is difficult to think they were ignorant of all that came to Brahms from the medieval world.

Nor is that precisely what Edward Canby wished to imply, for no one supposes total ignorance of that subject or that music on the part of the older commentators. But study from the page is one thing; practical experience through performance very much another. Thus it is in performance, the 'ultra-familiarity' that comes from frequent performance, that reveals, sometimes in a sudden flash, the real and deep-penetrating influences upon a composer in relation to another and older musical culture, or set of cultures. And it comes not only here, in the expected, predict-able places, in the case of Brahms and the old Church composers in the vocal music; for once the scent is picked up, the trail exposed and initially followed, it leads ultimately not to one end but to many, not here only but everywhere. Thus, taking from the vocal music, and in the first place perhaps specific vocal works, one sees the 'influence' at work all over. The voice-leading, part-writing, textural simplicity-cum-complexity, in the chamber music, even at times in the orchestral writing (Fourth symphony, for example), are everywhere under that same potent and fructify-ing influence. Thus one soon understands that the familiar idea of Brahms using classical forms for modern purposes is but a part of the story, and that the old ecclesiastical music in its blending and mixing in the nineteenth-century context of Brahms's par-ticular creative faculty was no less important; and that it does not, ultimately cannot, end there.

Here again one comes face to face with the nineteenth century's romantic trafficking with medievalism; again the hint of William Morris socialism in Brahms. But Brahms was too strong-minded, too intellectually robust, to fall for the vague day-dreaming and sentimentalizing of the Morris type. W. B. Yeats called William Morris 'the happiest of the poets', and indeed Morris does appear to have been happy in some kind of blissful innocence, dreaming of things that catch the imagination of those of today's young people who look for some deeper sense of community in a society they feel to be hostile, as when he spoke of 'the house that would please him where there would be some great room where one talked to one's friends in one corner and ate in another and slept in another and worked in another'. But Johannes Brahms was not a 'happy poet', and despite his reverence for the music of medieval times could not look there to some dream of innocent, childlike bliss, for in him moved the modern restless spirit and he too was victim of the Hegelian 'tragedy of consciousness'. For him the old music and the ways of life it represented were not resolution of the modern problem but something from which one must learn through study in order to increase the scope and technical richness of an art essentially contemporary, an art which for all its gesture towards classical order and restraint was ever dyed with romantic unrest and the romantic awareness that happiness is not a man's portion in this life. The quiet, resigned melancholy his music so often expresses was in no sense a nostalgia for lost Eden, nor hope for its recovery through some return to innocence; nothing either of that familiar romantic belief in the divinity of childhood uncorrupted by the contamination of the adult world.

Though Brahms loved children, there is no evidence that he saw them in the Wordsworth-Schumann-Jean-Paul Richter sense, but simply as children, delightful in themselves but signifying no more. He was taken in neither by the childhood of the person nor the childhood of the world. His medieval allegiances were purely musical; but as such they informed more than may appear upon the surface.

There was of course a strong precedent: Beethoven too had gone back to the old Church composers and learnt, for his 'third period', new ways of voice-leading and part-writing. But Beethoven by then had passed into spiritual penetration far beyond any achieved by Brahms—or by Wagner—and so the results of such study were, for him, very different. Nor did Brahms come late to that study, as Beethoven did, and had to because of the time in which he lived. For Brahms, initiation came early, with his childhood tutor, Pastor Geffcken, who introduced him to the old Protestant chorales and Church music. But deeply Protestant though he was, both by temperament and training, because of the dual religious life of Germany as a whole, he also made contact in his own time with the old Catholic composers and their music; and this also worked formatively upon him. Either way, his music in all forms more and more revealed the unarguable influence of a wide range of old music.

Yet as Edward Canby rightly concludes: 'The astonishing thing is that Brahms still sounds like Brahms! There is so remarkably little compromise—at least as we hear it.'

No compromise; an unshakable creative integrity, not in the least undermined by charges that at times he faked, for if and when he did resort to some species of 'faking' he did so not out of irresponsibility but precisely because of an almost too deep reverence for the exemplars of the past. In any case, all artists fake some-where, sometime. The very greatest, like Beethoven, only do it where it doesn't matter, and only in rare circumstances (which is one reason why they are great). But to say that any artist never fakes is to close the eyes and verge upon a species of uncritical hagiology. Again, composers like Brahms, who work loosely and broadly within established forms, especially sonata form (although in fact Brahms's forms are seldom as slavishly imitative as they have been made out to be), are more likely to be detected in faking than those who, like Wagner or Liszt, are seeking and have to create new and unfamiliar forms. No doubt Liszt often faked, and Wagner sometimes; but because the basic structure does not rely upon familiar procedures the effect is different. They had not the tradition of a convention to fall back on: Brahms had. There-fore 'fake' Brahms tends to stick out and will not pass unobserved.

Brahms was, whatever else, an honest composer. He did not take in others, and he seldom deceived himself, either technically or emotionally. The melancholy and resignation is as much a part of the reproach as the refusal to titillate or compose to catch the passing fashion only. He was a humanist realist for whom a facile vision of human happiness became more and more impossible, an escape into some dream of lost innocence unthinkable. He learnt the lesson early, and he did not again fall into a temptation to forget it. Maybe it was inherent in him, an inescapable condition imposed on him at his birth. Above all, after early tiltings with the infinite, he was profoundly aware of human limitation, his own not the least. He did not reach for godhead, as Beethoven through immense spiritual concentration, superhuman in its intensity, and Wagner through fierce dramatic gesture on a lower plane, both did. He trod the difficult stony path of men, his music human only, but deeply and enrichingly human in its honest strength and reflec-tive tenderness long before he approached the term of his active days. It is not everything; but it is quite definitely something. And it remains a reproach to all facile, unthinking, exhibitionist, evasive or self-deceiving art, of yesterday or of today. Huneker's judgment is ultimately justified.

6 The Two-way Split

In September 1862 Brahms went to Vienna, cultural capital of the German-speaking world, musical centre of all Europe. He went in the first place to promote himself and his arduously progressing reputation; but the results went much further than that. Vienna and Brahms found that, despite a few differences of taste and outlook, they liked each other. He remained an inhabitant of the Austrian capital for the rest of his life.

Hamburg to Vienna: the move in itself was significant. Perhaps upon the surface it may seem odd that this son of the solid North German earth, this staunch German patriot and liegeman of Bismarck, should have chosen Vienna as his home and domicile. One would more easily have seen him drawn towards Berlin; and maybe he would have been had Berlin been less culturally raw, crude, unsophisticated. As it was, Vienna, home of Mozart, the aging Haydn, Beethoven, Schubert, seemed for Brahms the most natural and predictable magnet. And indeed, if he never quite became a typical Viennese, with the tendency towards frivolity and sugar-sweet sentimentality as well as bitter-sweet nostalgia, he came to love the lighter music of Vienna, the waltzes and polkas, the street songs and café bands, and let it all seep deep into his mind and soul and come out again in guises not at all unrecognizable in his own compositions.

He came to Vienna from Hamburg, where he had suffered a major disappointment in being passed over for the post of conductor to the Philharmonic Society in favour of his former friend the singer Julius Stockhausen. He arrived in Vienna by no means obscure, though his music was still to gain wide familiarity there, for behind him was not only a body of work and the acclaim of several internationally regarded musicians, but also the sad affair of the 'Manifesto', tidings of which had percolated through all the musical world, and certainly to Vienna. Led by ironic coincidence, 1862 came in the middle of the clutch of years during which Richard Wagner was frequently in Vienna, vainly trying to revive his fortunes by arranging for a performance of *Tristan und Isolde* which he had written specifically for that purpose. The idea of *Tristan* as a pot-boiler may seem preposterous, even by Wagnerian standards: on the other hand, its vaguest possibility does indicate the range and potentiality of musical appreciation in the Vienna of the mid nineteenth century.

Though it was not specifically, not even generally, anti-Wagner, at least on Brahms's part, the 'Manifesto' had helped to make him, in certain musical quarters, infamous as well as famous.

It happened like this. In 1859 Schumann's old paper, the *Neue Zeitschrift für Musik*, achieved its twenty-fifth birthday. Since 1848 it had been edited by Karl Franz Brendel, a musical 'progressive' and supporter of the 'New Music' of the neo-German school centred at Weimar. And because most things in a complex and active world are confused, or are immediately made so if they are not of their own accord, a widening gulf was opened between the 'progressives' and the 'traditionalists'. It is an old story, and a disagreeable one; but it has to be told again, at least outlined in essence, because it bears directly upon the life and times of Johannes Brahms and because, like it or not, he was centrally embroiled in the deployment of its main forces and both received and returned a measure of fire in the journalistic cruiser sweeps which kept it going long after it should have sunk decently beneath the troubled waters.

The crisis came in 1860, when a group of young German musicians, Brahms and Joachim in the lead, took active objection to the wilder claims of the 'progressive' school, especially that their theories had been accepted by everyone who mattered in music. Some form of answer was to be expected, from some quarter on the other side; but the actual form it took was both injudicious and ineffectual. Who stirred the mixture first and strongest is hard at this range to discern. Probably it was Brahms: Joachim appears to have had his doubts, especially on practical grounds. 'There is much to be said against it from a worldly wise point of view,' he wrote to Clara Schumann in March; 'but I am anxious to repeat openly, in a short, dry and simple form, that which is known by my intimate friends, so that I may, once and for all, clear myself from the suspicion of cowardice.' Cowardice is a strange word in this context: Joachim might with more sense have restrained rather than encouraged those who yearned for a declaration of war which, in the arts as everywhere else, leads but to the loss of what one strives to preserve, usually through some triumph of the ridiculous. Whether Brahms pushed Joachim or Joachim pushed Brahms, it is clear that both were set upon their course, and others were set with them. In another letter, to Brahms this time, dated 15th May (1860), Joachim outlined the position as it then stood:

Rietz will join our protest on condition that we wait for a definite provocation. He thinks this is sure to occur at the Schumann Festival at Zwickau; because he considers it absolutely necessary to chastise the people who so insolently claim Schumann as one of their company. He has promised to write to me about it before long, and he takes the matter *seriously*, although he was not convinced, at first, that any good would come from it. The gist of his objections is that the people in Weimar would only imagine we were attributing an importance to them which they could turn to their advantage. He says they are played out in any case! But Rietz will join in, as I said, on condition that the Schumann Festival at Zwickau is used as a pretext, and *that the blow is deferred until then*. Hauptmann, Lachner and Hiller would also like to join in, in that case. I think that as we have delayed so long another three weeks will not matter.[1]

The 'plan', as most people could have foreseen and many did foresee, misfired, blew out, went all over. The 'Manifesto' itself,[2] which should have had many eager signatures, through some form of administrative incompetence was put on public show with only four—Brahms, Joachim, Grimm and Bernhard Scholz. The lack of signatures made what would have been miscalculation into near farce. Not one of the signatories carried the force and weight of reputation to formulate laws for the musical world, let alone virtually to dictate terms. The impact was minimal upon all but the four young men who had thrust their necks out and found them trodden on.

There is no doubting their sincerity. Certainly Brahms was utterly sincere, passionately convinced that he was upholding the great and noblest traditions of German art and German music. If he was also manœuvred, as much by himself as by anyone else, into a false and ultimately damaging position, at least he cannot be charged with charlatanism. What perhaps, like the others, he mistook was the difference between temperamental affinity or personal taste and true moral or aesthetic principles. He disliked the music of Liszt: many people disliked the music of Liszt. He distrusted the music of Liszt and Berlioz: many people not otherwise embattled or axe-grinding distrusted the music of Liszt and Berlioz, though very few were found to dislike the persona of the man Liszt. Brahms had direct experience both of Liszt's personal charm and of his generosity of nature. There is no call to charge him—or Joachim, who had still closer relationship with Liszt— with ingratitude or any commonplace fancies of that sort. But where the Manifesto was wrongly directed was the way in which it made unwarranted assumptions in taking the particular for the general, and where it imputed the small motives of unimportant hangers-on to artists of clear stature and significance. But none

[1] Bickley, p. 201.

[2] See Appendix.

of that would have mattered had it not offered precisely what the hangers-on on both sides needed and must have prayed for—a stick to beat their opponents with: a spoon to stir a dirty pot.

Brahms, by attaching his name to such a paltry document, such an obvious piece of blatant pamphleteering, so that all suggestions of pique and personal malice could never be wholly repulsed, made it certain that some of the mud would stick onto his music. And that did matter, for it was to become one of the fuses which set off the worst and most disreputable outburst of squabbling in the history of music.

If the charge is true that Brahms was immature in some of his music composed before 1860—in the D minor piano concerto, for example—the 'Manifesto' shows with startling clarity that as a man in the life of the world he was still the greenest of greenhorns. Yet maybe that too is part of him, part in another sense and on another plane, a part of his true strength, as in its own way it was part of Beethoven's strength—for as G. K. Chesterton somewhere remarked, it is the greenhorn who prevails when the all-knowing ones are taken in. Later on, Brahms was not to be taken in: he grew shrewd, canny, calculating and a bit of a sophister in his daily life and actions. Probably that also was a result of putting too quick a pen to the 'Manifesto'. He had learnt another hard lesson.

It had grown from within. After the Schumann disaster, Brahms's creative energy went to some extent underground. He felt the need for further preparation, less because of some conscious awareness of technical fallibility—youth that does not know technical shortcoming in the face of surging emotion will never come to anything—than because of the inner force of turbulence inside him, centred round but not exclusively dependent on the collapse of Robert Schumann and his ingrowing love for Clara, demanded of him some retrenchment and redisposition of the creative energies. He spent part of several years in the quiet German township of Detmold, where there was an independent court ruled over by an enlightened Princess Frederike. With periods in Detmold, Brahms alternated visits to Göttingen (where the unpropitious affair with Agathe von Siebold took place) and

Hamburg. He was growing up, both as man and artist; and, as always, the process was neither easy nor unvaryingly comfortable.

At Detmold, Brahms acquired practical experience as conductor. He was always a skilled and highly individual pianist; but as a conductor he had to find his way slowly and never achieved more than professional competence. Not that it signifies: there is no reason why a composer should be a distinguished executant, in any field. He may be; he may not be. For Brahms, it was something of a half-way mark.

At Detmold too he immersed himself in renewed study of the classical masters, going back also to the pre-classical period and learning from both all that by application and determination he could learn. Something of this study of the older music comes out in the two orchestral Serenades Brahms wrote at Detmold. These are often taken as tentative early experiments on Brahms's part in writing for orchestra, he taking a cautious way because he was not sure of himself. This I doubt: as I have said before, Brahms very early in his life acquired all the technique he needed to undertake any task to which he elected to address himself. Why then the unambitious (if that is the word) scope and nature of the Serenades? Most likely because the old-world atmosphere at Detmold simply turned his creative thought and fancy that way at a time when he was in any case absorbed in study of older forms and procedures.

The Serenades are frequently taken to refer back to the eighteenth century, and to the Mozartian practice. Yet this is quite superficial: there is nothing, absolutely nothing, of Mozart in either Serenade: and the style is neither *galant* nor noticeably easy-going but harks beyond the eighteenth-century 'social' music to the sterner, more full-bodied, idioms of the seventeenth or even the sixteenth centuries. Though the form and sound are both nineteenth-century Brahms, the 'tone' is from that older Germany which Bach knew and honoured. In nearly every way and in music of all kinds, Brahms by-passed the typical eighteenth-century productions, certainly everything pre-Beethoven in that century, everything, that is, pertaining to Mozart and most to Haydn. There is in Brahms some occasional hint of Haydn's rustic ways, but seldom more than a passing recollection; but there is scarcely a gesture towards Mozart anywhere. This is especially true of the Serenades, and so at the outset of his orchestral career also he set his sails upon his own chosen course.

With Beethoven the question is of course more subtle. Brahms's allegiance to Beethoven is declared openly and at once, in the First piano sonata; and he never wavered in that allegiance, although with growing maturity and deepening knowledge of life and art it became less obvious, more completely assimilated into the totality of his creative processes. Some touches of Beethoven have been noted in the D major Serenade, Op. 11, the first, the Beethoven of the septet mostly but of certain symphonic movements also. But Beethoven had already begun to undermine the rococo eighteenth century, and what of Beethoven there is in the Brahms is still further from rococo elegances. On the other hand, the most 'Beethovenate' section of the Brahms D major Serenade is the second scherzo with its hunting horn and general bucolic rumbustiousness. But this is the Beethoven who had heard Méhul (unless Méhul in fact heard Beethoven first, though that seems unlikely), and the direction is ultimately the same. Yet even here, the stamp of Brahms is stronger than anything, despite the passing echoes, and if proof of that is needed it may be found in the Horn Trio Brahms wrote a few years later in which both form and tone confirm the total, unmistakable and continuing 'Brahmsism' of his compositions. Always in Brahms there are traits in an early work which are developed and consummated in a later one.

The D major Serenade is in fact a 'big' work, for all that it has a conventionally slight name. It uses the full resources of the contemporary symphony orchestra, and it passes in its six movements through formal and expressive reaches of deceptive scope and range. In fact the D major has many of the characteristics in orchestral guise of the B major piano trio in its original form, with the same virtues of direct and spontaneous expression and the same faults of long-windedness and some confusion of parts and aims. In both one cannot mistake the true, natural voice of a young composer of genuine individuality. However much of someone else there may be, the unavoidable impression is of young Brahms; and familiarity with later Brahms only serves to confirm it.

In a sense, though, the Second Serenade, in A major, Op. 16, is even more illuminating. Or would be if the original version had not been suppressed by the canny composer. The 'reduced' version, for what is virtually chamber orchestra, was published in 1875, and is that which we know and play (sometimes) today. Its character is given by the omission of violins in the scoring; and as with the D major there is no attempt at concision and economy. In the revision of the B major trio, Brahms did take his expansive young self in hand, and generally tightened the structure. In the A major Serenade he tightened the scoring but apparently left the thematic structure intact. Here again though, there is, in both Serenades, evidence of young Brahms's uncertainty over the form in which he should cast his musical material. The D major existed as a sketched-out octet (thus probably referring back to Schubert as well as Beethoven in the original idea), and the A major was certainly in existence in some form in 1858, for Clara Schumann refers to it in a letter to Brahms from Vienna, dated 20th December. He had apparently sent Clara a bundle of works for her approval. Indeed, this letter is revealing of the whole relationship, personal and artistic, between Brahms and Clara at this time. It is worth quoting at length:

> I should have been glad to send back your things sooner but I was unable to do so because I wanted to get more than a superficial knowledge of them. You know that the reading of a score is not an easy matter for me, and it takes me some time. Yesterday and today I have at last succeeded in having a few hours alone, and now to my joy I know everything thoroughly. But I cannot summon up the courage to write to you in detail about them. All the same I will try to imagine that things are still as they were before, and that I can tell you all that my heart feels with complete confidence. You know that I can say little that does not come from my heart. It is here that the music makes its first appeal, and when it has captivated me I can begin to think about it. What charms me most is the Serenade. I liked it from the opening bars and think it sounds exquisite. The

second motif forms a beautiful contrast to the first and when I once got beyond the progressions in the third, fourth, fifth and sixth bars I felt perfectly happy. When the bassoons and the clarinets come in I begin to warm up and continue to do so more and more until the D flat major is reached, when on pages 14, 15 and 16 the piece proceeds with wonderful subtlety and depth. From there onwards to the A major and the last pp. is heavenly, but I cannot get accustomed to the return to the first motif by means of the organ point in A. According to natural law ought not the organ point to have been on E? I say 'natural law', because no other can be considered when natural feelings are so peremptory—to me it sounds insipid. The end with its return to the second motif and its wonderfully sweet conclusion on A major is again very beautiful. How delightful the oboes are, and then the basses with the second motif. What strikes me as so ingenious is the triplet movement with the four quavers which pervades the whole—how powerful the effect must be in the fortissimo passage in the middle! In short I can only compare the effect of the whole with that of the most beautiful, which is the D major Serenade. But I find the development in this one much more successful. Is this Serenade to be given any more movements? [1]

What Clara saw was certainly incomplete, and even more certainly not what we know today. In between much happened to the A major Serenade, probably to its general advantage. As things worked out, it is not now unreasonable to see the two Serenades as complementary—the two aspects or facets representing light and dark, the D major a day piece, the A major a night piece: morning and evening anyway. Whichever you may choose one thing seems clear enough: Brahms's two Serenades have been underrated, not only by students of Brahms who thus mislead themselves into thinking of him orchestrally as the formidable *maestro* of the four symphonies and the three later concertos (upon which system of accountancy it is necessary to dismiss the D minor as 'immature', which leads to still more trouble), but no less by the larger musical

[1] Litzmann, vol. 2, p. 91.

public who are consequently led into missing out on some of his most attractive work. Biggest is best is not an unimpeachable principle of art.

That many of Brahms's early compositions experienced difficulty in finding their true form and physical outlet may not have been due simply to indecision and lack of confidence on the young composer's part. The three big piano sonatas indicate that he neither doubted nor lacked power of execution when he knew just where he was going and what he was doing. Another and more fruitful explanation is that as he progressed and became more and more aware of the dual nature of music in the nineteenth century, centred on the poles of the abstract and the illustrative (loosely speaking), he felt pulls which for the time being left him perplexed and uncertain. That is most likely why the D minor piano concerto, both the Serenades, the Piano Quintet, and the C minor Piano Quartet, as well as the First symphony, all went through various stages of evolution and virtual mutation before achieving birth in the form we now know. His habit of regularly making piano [1] arrangements of his orchestral works and many of his chamber compositions was no doubt in the first place practical and in accord with the taste or practice of the times when before the age of radio and recordings the piano reduction was the means by which orchestral and operatic music was able to be widely played and understood. But it may also have been a deliberate (or possibly subconscious) act of revealing the abstraction in the music's structure and evolution, for in the change of media from orchestra or instrumental group to piano the basic thought and bone structure are laid bare.

Abstract music, of which in fact there is comparatively little, exists independently of its means of performance. The prime examples are Bach's *Art of Fugue* and *Musical Offering*, left in open score, and the nearest we have come to pure musical thought. But a great deal of Bach's music in the instrumental and orchestral fields is essentially abstract, even where the instrumentation is specified. That is why Bach himself could transcribe his music with

---

[1] Two or four hands.

an easy conscience (in fact without being aware of an issue of artistic conscience at all), and also why we can transcribe his music for ourselves so long as we truly understand it and do use it simply for our own egotism. Schweitzer, inveighing against the 'evil transcribers', was too obsessed with his theories of Bach's musical symbolism in the cantatas to see the implications of the abstract nature of Bach's instrumental works. And of course, 'abstract' music is not music without feeling or emotion, 'head-music' only: the abstract is as much an expressive concept as any other; it depends upon who uses it and how. Nor is it true to say that classical art tends towards abstraction but romantic art does not. Much is determined by the age in which it appears. Nineteenth-century Romanticism did not embrace a strong element of the abstract, and in its most comprehensive and far-flung form, as in the music dramas of Wagner or the instrumental and choral/orchestral music of Liszt, it is hardly 'abstract' at all. But for Brahms, poised between the classical and the romantic in the nineteenth-century context, with the classical allegiance but the Romantic impulse, the problem was always different and always acute.

That particular problem culminated in Schumann and came to resolution in Brahms. But it did not begin with either. It gathers force in Haydn and even more in Mozart, and makes open issue in Beethoven.

The claim that Brahms's achievement in orchestral symphony was to reconcile the opposing claims of the classic and the romantic, of the lyric and the dramatic, is not to be substantiated. Beethoven had already faced that problem and solved it by force of creative genius in the *Eroica* symphony and still more in the Fourth, which far from being a reversion to the style of Haydn and Mozart is a consummation of that of the *Eroica*. In Beethoven there is constant duality brought to unfailing resolution, not through side-stepping or backing down, but through the most potent heat of creative fusion. Thus in Beethoven classic-romantic, abstract-concrete, subjective-objective are at once clearly defined and creatively released. For Brahms the position was different. True, he did achieve fusions in a way and manner of his own, adding to the general store of musical development; but it was not in the plain, straightforward sense of Beethoven, any more than his music repeats the broad, simple tonic-dominant swing of Beethoven's characteristic middle-period style. Indeed, the way in which Beethoven, moving far away from his central tonality because he so unambiguously insists upon it, contrasts with Brahms's frequent tonal ambiguity is musical symbol of psychological bias.

Confusion has arisen because Brahms has been appointed the official heir and legatee of Beethoven, whereas in fact at most significant points, at those where he is most himself and most truly creative, Brahms went in directions virtually opposite to those of Beethoven. Beethoven's direction led ultimately only to one end—his own, that of the third period sonatas and quartets which, apart from a few technical devices, became in reality a dead end for nearly a hundred years. In saying as much, one implies of course no diminution of Beethoven's overwhelming achievement: rather the contrary, for Beethoven went so far in spiritual penetration and musical evolution to match it that he effectively left the soil barren from temporary exhaustion. Beethoven exhausted the soil in which he worked much as T. S. Eliot demonstrated that Virgil had exhausted the literary epic, so that the soil had to lie fallow for many years before it could be profitably tilled again. In the case of music, the land was not left to lie fallow—which is one reason why the nineteenth century is littered with musical debris of composers who came to grief on the giant Beethovenian rock, which they could not avoid but could not emulate. And some of these were left by Johannes Brahms—idle to deny it, though precisely how and why he left them has usually been misunderstood.

Thus Brahms's real achievement was not to continue where Beethoven left off, or any commonplace nonsense of that kind, but to reinforce and recharge the then established forms of German music by looping back to the old medieval music and the complex polyphony of the pre-classical period, and welding what he learnt there into the framework of sonata form. True, Beethoven had indicated the way here too, in his last works; but few understood those exact implications—which is why the last works of Beethoven were considered 'obscure' and 'difficult' until well into the twentieth century (the technical difficulties were for years used as a 'blind' for lack of creative understanding)—and for most of the nineteenth century the influential Beethoven was the 'second period' Beethoven, up to around 1814, and thus before he had used the whole of himself and put out the fullest force of his genius. Though late Beethoven laid a certain mark upon the nineteenth century, it was not until the evolution of modern music that its full impact was revealed, its total significance recognized. Third period Beethoven belongs essentially to the modern world.

Brahms belongs to the modern world too, though in a more limited sense. Brahms was both spiritually and technically a modern man in his own times; but Beethoven is modern in all times. Brahms is not for his own time only, like the myriad small fry who proliferate in any age: he is larger, more enduring, more universally orientated than that. But he cannot be anything if he is tied to Beethoven's coat-tails and apron-strings. He does not even make sense if he is so tied, for he in truth represents one prong of the two-way split in music after the death of Beethoven; the other prong represented by Richard Wagner of course.

Of course. If Brahms represented the formal and traditional side of music in the nineteenth century, Wagner represented the dramatic force and expressive power of music caught up directly in the huge evolutionary thrust of the age. Though both revered and appeared to start from Beethoven, in fact neither owed him more than reverence when they looked into their true hearts. For Brahms some aspects of sonata form; for Wagner some hint to be followed of the combination of voices and orchestra from the finale of the Ninth symphony. But no more: at bottom, nothing more than that. It would be quite wrong to suggest that at the end of his life Beethoven laid a false trail; but it can hardly be denied that he had advanced by then so far down a path uniquely his own that none but he could tread there, so that the trail he left could not be followed until the better part of a hundred years of human and artistic evolution had supervened. Thus was Eliot's assertion of the interaction of past and present most potently vindicated in the art of music through late Beethoven.

And because Beethoven had to all intents exhausted the soil in which he worked, the two-way split became unavoidable. Each path could, and did, lead to new gains and fresh discoveries; but neither could in any sense be seen as a continuation of Beethoven in any but superficial respects. If Beethoven had showed one way in respect of form and another in the expressive power of music, both, in so far as they stemmed from Beethoven at all, took the cue from second rather than third period Beethoven, and therefore from what Beethoven himself had outgrown. This is particularly true in the case of 'sonata form', which many post-Beethoven composers tended to use as though it was an *a priori* principle instead of a precise way of thinking and feeling in music and without creative insight into its overall relevance. Unfortunately for those who tried to uphold sonata form as the righteous tradition in composition, its so-called laws were only formulated and codified by pedagogues long after the event, so to say. For neither Haydn nor Mozart was sonata form rigid and prescribed, a rule-of-thumb procedure to be adhered to, and for Beethoven it was a starting point rather than an end in itself. It was, as the American pianist and scholar Charles Rosen has insisted, essentially a free form, as free as the Ballade for Chopin or Schumann's *Carnaval*.

All attempts to relate Beethoven's last works to the laid-down 'laws' of sonata form only show that those who make them understand nothing of the true principles of Beethoven's creative processes. Sonata form as an active principle in musical composition was killed off by the codifiers. Whoever wrote the book of sonata form, it was certainly not Haydn, who is generally credited with having 'fathered' the classical style in symphony and string quartet; and just as certainly Mozart had not read it. As for Beethoven, he least of all paid attention to the textbook, and the older he grew the less attention did he pay to any preconceived ideas of form. As Charles Rosen pointed out, anticipated by Donald Tovey, early Beethoven may appear to conform to the principles of sonata form, but late Beethoven returns more to the free style of Haydn and Mozart. But this is in one sense to reverse priorities, for those principles were in fact deduced long afterwards from early Beethoven and certain aspects of Haydn and Mozart: at the time there

were no such 'laws' to hinder the free flow of the creative imagination.

In another important respect too the composers of the expansive
and romantic nineteenth century reversed the central principles
of Beethoven's art. Where Beethoven had moved more and more
towards concentration and compression, the romantics tended to
a diffusion and loosening of form. The vast time spans of Wagner's
music dramas and Bruckner's symphonies (about the only thing
the two had in common despite Bruckner's enrolment in the barren
warfare as the 'Wagnerian' symphonist) were totally opposite to
Beethoven's almost nuclear compression of essence and energy.
The crunch probably came in the celebrated confrontation between
Mahler and Sibelius, when Mahler declared that the symphony
should 'be like the world; it should contain everything', to which
Sibelius retorted that on the contrary it was the discipline and logic
of the symphony that most appealed to him. And indeed Sibelius
with his constant move towards compression and concentration of
both form and utterance (the two of course cannot be separated)
showed himself to be akin to Beethoven in this respect, if in no
other, and opposed to nineteenth-century diffusion and expansion
leading often to magniloquence.

Much nonsense has been talked about Sibelius's indebtedness
to Beethoven; but it is true that Sibelius's musical mind did move
on a parallel course to Beethoven's in this at least, and that he was
the first symphonic composer since Beethoven to seek concentration rather than diffusion of symphonic form. And in so doing
Sibelius brought the orchestral symphony back into accord with the
modern idea, put it into step with contemporary thought and feeling, by-passing nineteenth-century romantic indulgences and
discursions.

The first discursively romantic composer was probably Schubert; but Schubert, partly through the shortness of his life, its
abrupt termination before he had time to carry music all the way
into his enchanted regions, is an isolated case. The 'Great' C
major symphony of Schubert with its 'heavenly lengths' is the
classic example of the discursive symphony, burgeoning forth out
of Schubert's uncomplicated and generously impelled nature,

reflecting the dawn and golden sunrise of Romanticism when the dew was fresh on the grass and the sun unclouded by later despairs and self-questionings. The story that Schubert towards the end of his life wished to take lessons in counterpoint is usually accepted as evidence that he knew his technical limitations and was desirous of rectifying them.

But I am sure Sir Neville Cardus is nearer the mark when he argues that what Schubert was really after was the kind of formal erudition that would be advantageous to him in the matter of obtaining an official appointment. Schubert as a self-conscious contrapuntal composer makes about as much sense as Brahms as a vagrant (also Cardus's word [1]) one. Nothing in Schubert suggests, or ever could suggest, that he would have been an improved composer through some acquisition of learned counterpoint.

Yet counterpoint is the key to all that makes Brahms. Contrapuntal skill and resource was not only his particular contribution to music nominally written in sonata form—it is also what enabled him to avoid appearing as a merely sub-Beethoven composer, formally speaking. For Brahms it was not sonata form but counterpoint and mastered polyphony that released his creative force and gives his best music its unmistakably individual stamp—counterpoint going back both to and beyond Bach as initial impulse and starting point. Where Brahms can be accused of having been a merely academic composer, where he can occasionally be detected in the act of faking, of covering his tracks when inspiration cools, is less in his falling back upon the more or less imaginary rulers of 'sonata form' as in his recourse to the spinning out of guileful counterpoint to no clearly revealed creative end.

When music split after Beethoven, and largely because of Beethoven, going one way with Brahms, another with Berlioz, Liszt, Wagner, the cleavage was bound to appear more real and more decisive than it really was. No doubt there was a genuine conflict of ideas and ideals: once Beethoven had opened the sluice-gates and unleashed an immense power both of form and expressive force, there was inevitably such a general inundation that those

[1] *Ten Composers.*

who followed him were obliged to seek refuge on whatever islands they could find and reach, and were likely to glare at each other in a certain enmity, each claiming that their own piece of dry earth was in fact the mainland. It was built into the overall situation, for Beethoven was not only the mighty giant of music but symbol of all those new forces of human consciousness and human aspiration released directly by the French Revolution but in fact the result of the sudden evolutionary forward thrust that came with the expanding nineteenth century, with what in effect was the birth of the modern world.

The arts, music included, maybe in Germany music foremost, were deeply involved in the new evolutionary movement; and as always happens at such times, when new directions have to be taken, when traditions break down and have to be replaced, it does not go all one way but leaps in many directions at the same time, the conflicting pulls between those who believe that all advance must come from deeper understanding of the past and those who proclaim that the past is dead and all must spring forward on a wholly new basis. It is not a question of conflict between those who cling obstinately to a vanished past and those who will to go forward—that is always a minor quarrel and always a barren one—but between different ways of going forward, of how best to answer to the onward thrust of evolutionary progress. All true art is progressive: reactionary art is always moribund and does not in fact answer to the name of art at all. And in the nineteenth century, with its conscious, and in the context inevitable, belief in progress, the minority pockets of reaction never had a chance anyway

In the perspectives of time, we can see that Brahms as well as the Wagner-Liszt faction was progressive, in the deep and meaningful sense of the term. Brahms would certainly have thought himself so, in the world in which he lived and worked. His outlook was essentially contemporary. He took great interest in all that was going on around him, in science, in thought, in literature, in politics. For him it was never a question of progress versus reaction, but of the best way to progress. And because of his inherited and acquired temperamental caution and prudence, it was inevitable that he should have chosen the path of springing forward from the firm basis of the past. With the ultra conservatives, in music the Leipzigers who fossilized after the death of Mendelssohn, he had no sympathy.

It is not at all surprising, and in no way passing coincidence, that Brahms was early on claimed by both the 'progressives' and the 'conservatives', or that he should have fallen foul of both on account of imagined apostasy. Here, as everywhere else, he followed a middle way, less from conscious choice than from the necessity imposed by his own nature and temperament. Not for him Blake's vision that the pathway of excess leads to the palace of wisdom. He left both the ecstasies and the sufferings of that path to the importunate Richard Wagner, who accepted it with reluctance, grumbled about it frequently, but in the end could not escape from it. Brahms's art was never for him a burden and a penance from which he prayed for release, as with Wagner: his own art was more comfortably worn; not wrenched from him as by some implacable force of destiny, but a natural and inevitable emanation of his being, accepted with a combination of humility and a sense of the large responsibility laid upon him. The fundamental difference between Brahms and Wagner is partly aesthetic; but far more it is rooted in the differing pressures of the evolutionary process in the era of its most vital and modern forward thrust. One might call Brahms and Wagner the negative and positive poles of evolutionary progress in the nineteenth century, provided one recognizes that both are essential to the full flow of creative energy. Both were certainly essential to the evolution of music after the titanic force of Beethoven, who contained in himself both positive and negative poles, the two fused together ultimately in a supreme peak of creative art.

Thus music divided after Beethoven, in order that it might gather new and revitalized energy. As I say, the split was inevitable: music could not in the circumstances have gone solely one way or the other. It was not so much that music in the nineteenth century needed the restraining hand of Brahms to offset the wilder and headier fancies of Wagner, or the courageous fight of Wagner to counter the stern and prudent disciplines of Brahms, as that it required both to fulfil itself in all its departments. Sometimes the age, in the familiar cliché, produces the man. It had produced

Beethoven. Now it produced two men, each complementing the other. In another sense and a different context it had produced Haydn and Mozart contemporaneously.

But it did not end there; was not left at that. Into the cauldron came the evil catalyst of a power-seeking critic, Eduard Hanslick. If it had not been for Hanslick, the dishonoured and dishonourable squabble between the Wagner and the Brahms factions would probably have been long forgotten and never have done more than ripple the surface of the musical world. Brahms and Wagner were not personal enemies: though they did not particularly care for each other as men, they respected each other's work. Brahms in particular maintained a lifelong interest in what Wagner was doing, and was invariably put into a bad temper in the presence of Wagner's detractors, saying that it was not Wagner but misrepresented Wagner that was the corrupting influence. Wagner for his part was cooler towards Brahms's music, but certainly did not despise it. The story of Wagner's remarking after hearing Brahms's Handel Variations that they showed what could be done in the old forms by someone who really understood them, may or may not be apocryphal; but even if it is, it probably represents Wagner's feelings.

But Hanslick would have none of this. Hanslick was bigoted and ignorant. Though a gifted and often graceful writer, he was a bad critic who would see only what he wanted to see and continually twisted facts to suit his preconceptions. He knew only a little music, and did not always understand what he did know. Old music was beyond him, and he believed that in his last works Beethoven had overstepped the bounds of musical decency. He hated the 'New Music' and was quite unscrupulous in his denunciations of it. His reward was a position of virtually unchallenged power in Viennese music circles—and the friendship of Brahms.

Brahms met Hanslick soon after he had settled in Vienna. The two men became fast friends. It must have been something in Hanslick's personality that attracted Brahms, for it cannot have been his musical and critical abilities. Brahms saw through these from the beginning, and was in the habit of making quite disparaging remarks about Hanslick's obtuseness—which Hanslick can only have tolerated for the advantage in his power campaignings Brahms's friendship afforded him. Hanslick in fact was a man who tried to call 'halt' to all progress: he went so far as to say that Beethoven's late works had given Art the sombre warning: thus far and no further. One might ask when Art ever said, or even temporarily implied, such a thing. Only Hanslick can give answer.

Hanslick was not always wrong. If he had been he would have got nowhere. Mean and spiteful little critics who know nothing are easily disposed of. Hanslick frequently made sound judgments, and even when he did not he often wrote at length with a lucidity which deceived many into believing that he did. He represented the core of diehard reaction in an age of considerable confusion, when many were afraid of all change because they felt the foundations shifting under their feet. Hanslick too hated change and feared progress. He attacked the 'New Music' ostensibly because he feared that it constituted a destroying danger to the art of music as he understood and honoured it. But he also attacked it because such an attack gave him a position of influence in Vienna; and in that he was a hypocrite, at least a self-deceiver. He had to take sides because he longed for power, and those who do not join intemperately in the going battle are inclined to be by-passed by both sides.

To read Hanslick today, when the smell of powder and the clang of shot are long behind us, is not wasted time, for he was a man of some taste and discernment, to some extent a man of principle, though wrong-headed. But it is impossible to avoid the sense of wilful bias and deliberate misrepresentation, so that when one comes upon some passage of penetration and eloquence the suspicion that all is not what it seems, and is meant to seem, and that Hanslick is up to something, cannot be avoided.

Hanslick's championship of Brahms seems at first to have been noble and selfless. Until one knows what is behind it. He seems to have understood Brahms's music, and he is not above doing a sharp critical job whenever he feels that Brahms has slipped a rung or two. But his support of Brahms was ultimately something for which Brahms himself cannot have been pleased. Brahms put himself into a false position with the business of the 1860 'Manifesto'. Hanslick made sure that Brahms could not escape from it. Hanslick claimed that his quarrel was not with Wagner but with the legion of vituperative Wagnerites. He may have thought it was true, but his writings do not encourage us to believe it. After Wagner had died, Hanslick made a kind of gesture of reconciliation to the inescapable Bayreuth ghost. But it does not ring true. Hanslick, we must suspect, was simply bowing to the inevitable. Once Wagner was safely out of the way, his work done, his battle over, Hanslick seems to have reached the old conclusion that if you cannot beat them join them—at least look as though you have joined them.

How 'bad-tempered' Brahms put up with Hanslick is one of music history's minor wonders. He even said that he would have to become a Wagnerian in order to pick a quarrel with the anti-Wagner faction in Vienna. Yet he remained on terms of intimacy with Hanslick, although it became increasingly clear that far from supporting Hanslick's theories and prejudices Brahms was against virtually all of both. It must simply have been that Brahms found Hanslick an agreeable man and a worthy friend. At the end of his life Brahms was still meditating on his friendship with this fellow. In a letter to Clara Schumann he declares himself perplexed by it still, 'seeing that we each have such very different points of view', but finding great personal virtue in the venerable critic. A curious business. Its importance to a study of Brahms is really to note that Brahms was certainly Hanslick's true friend, but was not taken in by Hanslick's critical imbecilities. It matters because it shows that Brahms was not prepared to allow his name to be used as a stick to beat Wagner. Or if he allowed it, it was because he couldn't help it, and did nothing to encourage anything so disreputable.

Now that all is quiet and both Brahms and Wagner are accepted as classics, have virtually assumed the dignity of ancients, we can forget Hanslick and see how the two great composers really stand face to face. I take it as in no way significant that there are a number of echoes of Wagner in Brahms's music; a passage here, and turn of phrase there, a progression somewhere else. That is simply because there was inevitably a certain common currency in German

129

music of the day, and a little of it was sure to be common to even such apparent opposites as Johannes Brahms and Richard Wagner. Yet were they after all really such opposites? Temperamentally, yes. But musically? It must certainly appear so, but for one work *Meistersinger*. How often do theories and opinions about Wagner founder upon the solid and irremovable rock of *Die Meistersinger*; for *Meistersinger* is not a 'sport' among Wagner's works, not a deviation from the norm, but something central and essential to Wagner's creative genius, something without which great ranges of his other works could never have come into being at all. *Meistersinger* is not only the complement to *Tristan* as day is to night, as diatonicism is to chromaticism, as the active is to the passive, the mobile to the immobile; it is the open declaration of the fount from which at least half of Wagner's genius in any context arose. And *Die Meistersinger* inhabits and celebrates precisely that German art and world which Brahms's music inhabits and celebrates.

Die Meistersinger is old-world in setting but modern bourgeois in feeling and sentiment. And so is much of Brahms. Why those who hailed Brahms's First symphony as 'the Tenth' could not see that the big tune of the finale was much closer in tone and spirit to *Meistersinger* than to any part of Beethoven is beyond credulity, especially since there is a perfect clue in the brass chorale which sounds a direct echo from *Meistersinger*. This should not be taken as further evidence of Brahms's 'plagiarism', the sort of trumped-up charge advanced only by those whose grasp of the obvious seems to them unimaginable revelation, but simply as the normal and natural working of a general currency of musical language in a particular time and circumstance. Nor is the *Meistersinger* theme in Brahms's A major violin sonata, Op. 100, more accidental or not accidental than any other reference of the kind, either from his own compositions or from somebody else's. The relationship between accident and non-accident, between conscious and unconscious, chance and teleology as it might be, in all such cases is complex and subtle: it cannot be given a short snap answer. So the relationship between Brahms and Wagner as the two leading representatives of German music in the nineteenth century is also complex and subtle. The idea that they were simply at loggerheads is infantile and irrelevant—as infantile and irrelevant as the petty squabbling that surrounded them in their joint lifetimes.

Hanslick was not the originator of the quarrel and certainly not its singular perpetrator. The quarrel itself was carried on by innumerable parasites on the fringes of the musical world who, as parasites invariably do, formed themselves into warring cliques, covering their impotence by the loudness of their noise. The shame of Hanslick is that instead of using his position of influence to rout the idiot factions, he deliberately used it to further his own personal ends and fed flames a more honest man would have quickly doused.

Yet even the evil of Hanslick's factioneering brought forth good. Wagner originally intended *Die Meistersinger* as a direct attack on Hanslick, the figure of the crabbed critic, later Sixtus Beckmesser, named Hans Lich. But Wagner was true genius, and true genius is never spiteful, petty, malicious, but generous and open-hearted, not devoted to quarrelling. If Wagner seems as a man to have been aggressive, quarrelsome and largely insufferable, that was only upon the surface, and the artist in him, what mattered him that is, had that deep-down quality of generosity and good-will that is not only typical but essential in all major geniuses. And *Meistersinger* is its proof, not only in itself but even more in the manner of its transformation in Wagner's creative soul from the critic-baiting pamphlet of its origins into the warm human comedy that it became and is now forever. It was Hanslick not Wagner who was motivated by malice, impelled by rancour, full of the spirit of enmity and poison.

Brahms and Wagner meet on the common ground of *Die Meistersinger*, upon that firm German soil and proclaimed faith in German art and the German people that stretches far beyond narrow nationalism, mere chauvinistic rantings, or egotistical posturings, and reaches out to the universal human experience from the basis of a home soil and a just pride. From that common ground each went a separate way; or perhaps one might also say that each approached the common ground from different viewpoints. But whichever way you choose to phrase it, the ground is still common.

That Wagner should have distrusted Bismarck and the pan-Germanism he worked for while Brahms revered the man and strongly supported the idea is also no surprise and wholly in accord with the nature and character of each. Wagner may have appeared the loud-voiced German patriot, the ecstatic celebrator of blood and race; but that too was only to see upon the surface. The deeper Wagner, the social revolutionary of 1848 who fought at the barricades alongside the anarchist Bakunin, whose ideals though windy were essentially and truly democratic, this Wagner was of necessity bound to reject the German Empire of Bismarck with its conservative bent, its centralization of power and authority, its suppression of liberal thought and institutions. But Brahms, by nature conservative, bourgeois, constitutional, would just as naturally have gravitated towards the Bismarckian concept of a German State bound together by common social, economic and political ties, the sources of government vested in the German Emperor. All that we know of each man, through his music and his biography, indicates a division and direction of loyalty upon the planes that are in fact immediately revealed. Romantic Wagner would have thrust politics as he thrust music into new and rich fields of evolutionary aspiration; conservative Brahms, also romantic but restrained by prudence, would no less naturally have kept politics within established and recognized bounds, or at least those based upon firm establishment, as he kept music on a roughly similar course.

The dual aspect of Romanticism is not easy to define: it is in fact most completely revealed in the Wagner-Brahms confrontation. The evolutionary and the consolidatory; the existential and the academic; the Bohemian and the domestic. Yes; maybe. But all such only indicate directions in general, not the substance, the heart of the business. Only in the illumination of contrast can the full situation be understood.

Confusion is only increased by the conventional idea of Wagner the musical adventurer, breaking bounds and carrying art into new and heady realms, and Brahms the musical supporter of tradition and establishment; Wagner pushing chromatic harmony out so far that tonality comes under sentence; Brahms adhering to rightful tonality as well as to sonata form. But tonality was also exhausted by Beethoven. The entrenchment of music in tonality had meant a certain diminution of both melody and counterpoint. Beethoven in his last years had begun to free melody and counterpoint once more, bringing back into music the potency of the modes, of polyphony, of infinite malleability of line and texture. Tonality had served a memorable and an indispensable purpose, carrying music into and through one of its great periods; but its time was come and with it the time of sonata form of which it was an inescapable concomitant. And both Wagner and Brahms led the process forward. If there is nothing in Brahms so harmonically significant and fruitful as the opening of the *Tristan* Prelude, his music is still full of tonal ambiguities and harmonic fluxes. It may be claimed that the ambiguities and fluxes were the result of Brahms's temperament, his caution and prudence, his lack of forceful affirmation, *à la* Beethoven. But this will not carry conviction very far. What of Wagner? Were Wagner's subtilizations of harmony and underminings of tonality the result of caution, indecision, lack of positive force? It would take a bold man as well as a stupid one to argue so. The truth is that these harmonic and tonal evolutions were as necessary in the post-Beethoven musical world as the drastic modification if not the outright overthrow of sonata form, confidently so called and latterly discovered and worshipped.

It thus becomes clear that once we look under the obvious surfaces the music of Wagner and Brahms had after all a good deal in common and was by no means diametrically opposed. They were Johannes Brahms and Richard Wagner, two sides of the same creative and historical process.

7 The Metaphysics of Freedom

For gods freedom is absolute but for men it is limited and even relative. And men, the master self-deceivers, never cease to twist themselves in knots in the attempt to reconcile the idea of freedom with its inevitable limitation; to persuade themselves, that is, that limited freedom is reality and that such an idea is not a logical and metaphysical monstrosity. Yet men who aspire to true freedom must aspire also to be godlike and must banish finally all naïve and nonsensical notions as 'Freedom but . . .' There is no such thing as 'freedom but . . .': 'freedom but . . .' is the same as Henry Ford's 'You can have a car any colour you like so long as it's black.' 'Freedom but . . .' is the ultimate snare which reduces man to slavery and impotence from which there is no escape. For a religious man it leads to slavery to God, and for the atheist it leads to slavery to materialistic determinism. Awareness of limitation, the classical ideal, is not primarily concerned with freedom in the deepest existential sense and is therefore capable of releasing potentiality through recognition that the infinite is beyond the grasp of the human spirit and intellect. It is in this sense that Goethe's dictum that the master works through knowledge of his limitation has creative meaning. In not claiming or reaching out for the totality of freedom man may achieve superior things, for he does not deceive himself; but as soon as he opts for freedom and then qualifies it he trips himself on a fatal paradox of his own making and thus endangers and ultimately undermines all that he attempts, for he begins to confuse the actual with the real, the attainable with the unattainable, the dream with the symbol of what is dreamt.

The whole Romantic movement in its highest flights was a violent protest against human limitation. It was a massive gesture on the side of freedom against enslavement to determinism, and it failed and in the end collapsed into neurosis and despair because it asked questions it could not answer and came up against the harsh facts of human mortality and entrenchment in the finite. It asked why men are not gods, and when it found that the dream would not answer to the reality, it broke down in bewilderment and sought refuge in the ache of nostalgia for lost Eden that never was and never could be because evolution is irreversible and cannot be turned back upon itself. It asked whether man was an ape or an angel and came out on the side of the angels; but when it found that the ape was too strong after all, despite all efforts on the part of the angels, it foundered in delusions of false grandeur and rhetorical gestures and so made the rift even wider. It strove towards freedom and understood that freedom is the attribute of gods; but because men are not gods but must submit after all to mortality and limitation, it sought for a compromise that did not exist.

In reaching out towards freedom Romanticism represented the quarrel between the finite and the infinite in the human soul and psyche; but it never succeeded in resolving the conflict. The appeal of the Catholic Church to many of the late Romantics and post-Romantics, who tended to seek refuge in it in droves when they did not turn to some naïvely optimistic vision of a newly emergent science, was an attempt to escape from the despairs and frustrations of a longing for the infinite within a context all too finite.

For many the Catholic Church was both refuge and panacea for hopeless longings, through submission to the spiritual authority of temporal institution which brought release from subjective torment and the individual burden of freedom. But the Church, with its ritual and dogma and concept of authority, is itself a recognition of human limitation and mortal finiteness, with the Pope the arbiter of God's will on earth and the symbol of Christ's mediation between God and man. The Protestant Church, with its rejection of papal authority and its insistence on individual will to salvation coupled with the doctrine of predestination, never compelled the Romantic imagination in the way the Catholic Church did, partly because the splendour and richness of Catholic ritual made an emotional as well as a spiritual appeal.

Yet the element of authoritarianism, with its concomitant recognition of human limitation and fallibility, is a denial of existential freedom and so a diminution of the deepest and most potent meaning of the true Christian message and revelation, which is above all the most profound declaration of the burden and tragedy of ultimate freedom. Dostoievsky's Grand Inquisitor charges Christ with laying the intolerable burden of freedom on men and thereby showing no pity towards them. And Kierkegaard, a leading existentialist philosopher, came out resolutely against the hierarchical structure of the Church, declaring that 'officialdom is incommensurable with Christianity'.

Christian myth and legend (rather than Christianity itself) made a strong impact on the late Romantic imagination. Wagner, whom no one would take for orthodox religious man or church supporter, was continually haunted by Christian legend; and in *Parsifal* he too capitulated, not to official orthodoxy but to the emotional pull of distant symbology, his vital force and reaching for freedom of *The Ring* and the other great works of his full-blooded maturity finally exhausted. Wagner too had at last to submit to the finite and the mortal, though he cloaked it in the scented terms of religious rites and in so doing could not entirely avoid all suggestion of the religioso. Liszt's path was more direct, and in the end less compromising. Liszt in his later life became an honorary Abbé of the Roman Church; but unlike Wagner one does not feel that he tried to hide behind the redemptive power of the religious life. Wagner's last musical thoughts, in *Parsifal*, were infinitely subtle and infinitely potent; but his emotional life at the end was all too finite. Liszt's last musical thoughts, as I have said, prepared the ground for the emergence of modern music in the twentieth century; and emotionally he was one of the few who did not capitulate.

Brahms in all this, as in so much else, steered a prudent middle course. Though he was caught up in the Romantic spirit and in his young days made certain gestures on the side of the infinite, he was never prepared to let it go to his head or to allow himself to become involved in its more reckless excesses. His stolid, sane, level-headed Low German bourgeois nature and temperament kept him on a steady keel, even when, as at the time of the Schumann debacle, he might well have been excused some loss of stability. And as he grew older he made sure that nothing would throw him off balance. He never lost his head, never went overboard for any form of Romantic indulgence or wildness. And there is no possible doubt that such a course was for him deliberate, even calculated. He knew the hot and searing Romantic passions inside him all right; but he determined at an early age that passion should not rule him and that however deeply he felt he would never give way to it. In much of his music the strong conflict between passion and intellect, between heart and head, is clearly to be felt; is in fact the source of the musical conflict. But one seldom feels that the passion is ever likely to overrule the controlling mind. It was deliberate, but it was probably never all that difficult for him: his natural bent and bias of temperament laid down his course for him and he was seldom, after the Schumann business anyway, in much danger of being driven off it.

Brahms's attitude to the problem of freedom was enigmatic, but ultimately clear enough. If he seems at first sight to have been one in danger of falling into the 'freedom but . . .' trap, it soon emerges that he never was really tempted into making much of a gesture on the side of perpetrated illusion. Undoubtedly for him freedom was qualified; on the other hand, he never pretended that he was deeply involved in the Romantic quarrel between the finite and the infinite: he never aspired to godhead; he lived and worked as a man and in the full knowledge of human limitation. Nor had he any religious aspirations, and so did not fall for any form of religious illusion. Though he drew widely and skilfully upon the Lutheran Bible for the texts of many of his vocal works, the great Requiem at the head, he neither sought nor pretended to find religious consolations, still less religious panaceas, whether individual or institutional. His resigned stoicism, which grew more informing with his own advancing years, his disillusion and melancholy, carry him in many ways forward into the twentieth century and into a world analogous to that of Ernest Hemingway, emotional and intellectual in his case, emotional and physical in that of Hemingway.

Closer than Hemingway, though again more intellectual, Brahms seems to stand with the great poet of the Victorian age, Alfred Tennyson. W. H. Auden once said that Tennyson knew everything about melancholy and nothing about anything else. It was not true, but like many wilful exaggerations it contained a sharp thrust of truth. Upon the same level of insight it might be said also of Brahms. Like Tennyson, Brahms knew about a great deal more than just melancholy; but also like Tennyson, melancholy is certainly a prominent (to say no more) feature of his work. There is indeed a good deal of correspondence between Brahms and Tennyson; not only the melancholy, but the same involvement with the essential spirit of the age, the love of the past and of the ancient lays, the same doubts and uncertainties, the same scientific curiosity and political loyalism, the same appeal to mild-eyed sentiment in love-songs, the same romantic but unreckless aura, the same tendency to sentimentality, the same pride in good craftsmanship and immense skill in technique. Above all, the same relationship to the middle-class society of the times, though Brahms remained to the end a man of the people, neither courting nor willing to accept lordship in any form.

Intellectually, Brahms may seem nearer to Robert Browning; but Browning's strongly confident optimism, anathema to the modern age, sets him far apart from Brahms, at bottom a necessary and inescapable pessimist. But with Tennyson in poetry there is a whole lot in common with Brahms in music. Interestingly, the late W. J. Turner, a gifted poet and music critic of yesteryear, when discussing the colours suggested by the music of various composers, put Brahms down as 'dark red'. Does not that too seem appropriate to Tennyson, who at least seems to come somewhere between magenta and purple and thus confirms the correspondence with Johannes Brahms? And Tennyson, also like Brahms, was hardly a wild seeker after total freedom, either in life or art, least of all in both together.

In the attitude to freedom, Brahms declared himself early. In the early days, Joachim had adopted a personal motto, musico-philosophical: F-A-E—*frei aber einsam* (free but lonely); whereupon Brahms adopted for himself a slightly different but highly revealing one: F-A-F—*frei aber froh* (free but happy). Metaphysically, Joachim's motto was unexceptionable: free men are often lonely; the road of freedom is frequently a lonely one, inevitably a lonely one, one might say. But hardly Brahms's. 'Free but happy': it is a knotty problem of Teutonic metaphysics to understand why a man should be free *but* happy, as though the happiness deriving from freedom were a cause for astonishment. Nothing more indicates the direction and quality of Brahms's thought on freedom than the placing of the 'but' between freedom and happiness.

Of course one might say that it depends on what is meant by happiness. Joachim's loneliness as expressed in his motto might not necessarily lead to happiness in the ordinary, worldly sense; and maybe Brahms could persuade himself that to be happy as well as free was a notable achievement. It could even at sight be taken as a reference to his bachelordom, or might have been so taken later on. But at this time it is unlikely that he was confirmed in celibacy. He had probably already fallen for Clara Schumann; but Robert Schumann was still very much alive, no hints of the coming tragedy yet showing to his young friends (though they were there beneath the surface all right), and Brahms's feelings for Clara were not yet likely to provoke him to curious philosophy. No: it is not that either. Every pointer is to 'free but happy' as a direct and incontrovertible expression of Brahms's life-view, and one that was to be strengthened and confirmed rather than contradicted in the succeeding years. It tells us a great deal about him and his outlook; and if what precisely it tells us is everywhere confirmed in his music, that only serves to strengthen the force of the basic argument.

And indeed the musical force and relevance of the motto were as strong as the philosophic. It appears in several of Brahms's works, in one guise or another; but it is given a full working out and exposition, both musically and metaphysically, in the Third symphony, in F, Op. 90. This has sometimes (cf. Niemann) been called Brahms's 'Eroica', from the bold and open manner of its evolution, just as for equally observed reasons the Second has been called his 'Pastoral'. I do not myself set much store by such fancies, though in general terms they are inoffensive and certainly not idiotic as some applied names or nicknames are. But I have another idea for the F major. I have called it elsewhere Brahms's 'Credo' symphony, partly because it quite deliberately concerns itself with the F-A-F motto, but no less because of the resemblance of the opening to the Credo of Beethoven's *Missa Solemnis*, a resemblance so marked that once one has noted it seems almost as obvious as the resemblance of the C major piano sonata to the *Hammerklavier*. On the other hand, the implication of the music and the subsequent working out are so dissimilar that the correspondence can hardly have been other than immediate reference, if not a direct declaration of intent. Of course it may well in this case have been unconscious; but if so it still does not alter the fact or contradict the argument.

Brahms's musical mind was so seeped in the music of Beethoven that such references may well have come into it from the underside, so to say; but we cannot believe that what did come in that manner came also with its associated meaning. Thus if the Credo of the *Missa* came into Brahms's mind consciously or unconsciously as a musical intimation, it would have come also as the Credo and not in isolation from its context and relevance. I quoted the passages in a general book [1] and I quote them again now in a particular one, because I believe that this reference is the third element in the creative genesis of the F major symphony, the other two being the

[1] *An Adventure in Music*, p. 117.

note progression F-A-F with the A flattened, and the concomitant
frei aber froh. Here is the Brahms:

Example 1

And here the Beethoven:

Example 2

Yet even if the correspondence is not accepted, or I make too
much of it, the musical and philosophical progressions still justify
the appellation of the 'Credo' to this symphony. If one asks what
the F major is about, the unequivocal answer is: musically it is
about F-A-F, and philosophically it is about *frei aber froh*. It is
thus a particularly revealing example of Brahms's mature creative
processes, for it lays the abstract and the concrete in them side by
side, not only by implication but virtually by direct statement.
Overall the Third is the most *echt*-Brahms of all the symphonies,
and in many respects the most characteristic and illuminating of
all his major compositions. In its form and tonality as well as

philosophy and logic in the light of Brahms's particular and individual musical genius it is the complete and unchallengeable
expression.

The motto itself, informing all four movements, has a curious
feature, one that determines both the harmonic and tonal ground-
plan and ultimately the philosophic bias, thus:

Example 3

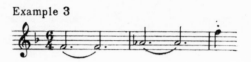

The flattened A provides the clue. The key of F major has a
natural bias towards flatness, and Brahms seems deliberately to
be pushing it as far as it will go in that direction. He begins
with what is in effect an incomplete arpeggio on F minor,
thus introducing a false relationship at the outset. Frank
Howes [1] demonstrated how Brahms's fondness for the progression

Example 4

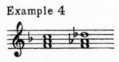

leads him to emphasize the 'flatness' of the key of F, making A
flat common to both F major and F minor, something which
Brahms further enforces in the F minor development of the first
movement and the minor-major alternations of the finale. The
tonal sequence of the middle movements also confirms this tendency—the second is in C turning to the minor, the third in C
minor with the trio in F flat. Thus, though the Third symphony
is a work of strength and in parts of sturdy exultation, the constant
pull towards the flat side of the tonic key gives it a feeling of stressed
ambiguity far removed from the directness and forthright clarity
of the classical period symphonies where the firm centre of the
tonic was always insisted upon. Frank Howes further asserts that
the musical argument of the Third symphony revolved upon the

[1] pp. 82–3.

possible flatness of the key of F and in particular of the inflection of the note A, working from the tonal ambiguity of the opening with the A flattened through A major (exposing the sharp side), C major-minor (natural-flat), and A flat major, finally resolving onto F major. This is no doubt true; but the symphony is also about the particular progression F-A-F, which Brahms had adopted as a musical-cum-philosophic motto and which he elected to explore in depth in this singular composition. But however you may wish to interpret it, either way or more likely both, here is the logical abstract of the F major symphony; the purely musical thinking within the complex structure. It is revealing because Brahms was a profound musical philosopher and here we have an unusually explicit sample of his thought processes.

But alongside the abstract logic of the F major symphony, the intellectual musical thought-process, lies the metaphysical impli- cation of F-A-F, translated into *frei aber froh*. Though Brahms has declared his happiness along with his freedom, though not apparently as a consequence of it, the flattening of the A in the musical process indicates some lack of clear affirmation, of any idea of hairy-chested optimism. Even here Brahms's pessimistic melancholy and stoical acceptance of the worst life has to offer can be felt. Obviously it would not be Brahms if it were not so; and this as I have said, is the most typical Brahms of all, his philosophical credo as well as his musical one.

Yet the note of sturdy independence is characteristic too—and it is in the symphony. In the finale one begins to feel that it will triumph after all, that the final swing into F major may be analo- gous in Brahmsian terms to Beethoven's irresistible swing into C major for the finale of his Fifth symphony. But no—the last bars are full of quiet acceptance, resigned calm of mind, all passion spent perhaps. This soft glow of gentle peace at the very end is indicative of the whole. Elgar, in notes for a lecture on the Third symphony given at the University of Birmingham, on 8th Novem- ber 1905, observed: 'Curious, all [movements] end *p* or *pp*.' There you have it: despite the 'heroic' tone of first movement and finale; despite the strength and lift of exultation, not one move- ment ends in triumph. Brahms was true to himself; he did not force, did not contrive a happy ending, or even a happy interlude, because at bottom he was not a man of victory but a man of sorrows.

Did he then deceive himself with 'free but happy'? Maybe he did, to an extent. Yet the evidence of the musical logic of the F major symphony suggest a different interpretation. Though he tasted the heady wine of Romanticism, and at times drank long and deep, his natural and ingrained sobriety prevented him from ever giving way to uncontrolled inebriation. 'I am the Bacchus who presses out this glorious wine for men, and makes them drunk with the spirit,' Beethoven had declared to Bettina von Brentano. The implied association with the gods is clear. Wagner would have understood: Wagner too reached for godhead, and so for true freedom. Wagner failed; but not Beethoven. Beethoven's last music is the human justification of the idea of absolute freedom of the spirit. Brahms never made the full attempt; never risked the leap, and the possible consequences of a heavy fall.

For Brahms, unlike for Beethoven and after him the headier Romantics, freedom lay in the recognition of limitation, as in the Goethean sense, nearer to the classical than to the romantic concept. Because men are not gods the wings of freedom are clipped, the vision set upon some practical, recognized horizon. The heroic mould in which Brahms was cast was human not super-human. He may engage in titanic conflict; but in the end his feet are kept upon firm earth. His religious and philosophic agnosticism led him to no heights of ecstasy or depths of terror. Here too, as in his music, the duality of his nature is revealed, the classic-romantic, subjective-objective pulls. And again, nowhere is this more openly outlined than in the Third symphony with its severe logical disciplines of musical thought confronting its warmth of texture, its expressive richness of polyphony, its generous lyric impulse in its contrasting 'feminine' themes.

With Brahms, however, these dualities, of masculine and feminine, classic and romantic, subjective and objective, are generally kept apart and are only to a limited extent cross-fertilizing. With Beethoven the opposing elements fused together in such a way and often at such a white heat that an immense force of dynamic power and creative energy was released. With Wagner, the sense of unbridled power within him led to a recklessness and importunate trafficking with the powers of darkness as well as light in a way that sometimes appalled him and has frequently appalled the world. But Brahms, with his prudent caution, natural from birth but reinforced by experience, was not going to allow the clash of disparate elements to give off uncontrollable sparks, to light fires that could not be doused. He was not going to let Dionysus out of the hutch—not unless he had a good tough chain ready to put the obstreperous god back into safe keeping again. Put it another way: Brahms was perfectly willing to climb mountains; but he always made sure the ropes were firmly secured behind him. He was willing to go on long and ardous journeys; but he took good care to consult a reliable map first.

To say that may be to set another mark against Brahms, to charge him with a kind of spiritual cowardice, to write him down among those who ultimately declined the real gambit and failed the test of their deepest humanity. For the essence of the divinely 'drunken' High Romantics was that they were willing, if not eager, to offer themselves as sacrifice on the altar of life and art, to accept if they had to the tragic consequences (Yeats's 'we do not begin to live until we conceive life as tragedy'), to be crucified on the obstinacy of the world. Brahms knew the force of tragedy, though not perhaps in the highest, the joyous sense; but he was not willing to risk more than he had to, did not fling out a vigorous challenge to the gods which sport with men, was not, in Wagner's term, at loggerheads with the world. He was, in short, the good bourgeois citizen in a firmly entrenched bourgeois world.

Yet if it does seem a mark against him, there may once more be another interpretation. For the majority of men, especially the majority of middle-aged men, Brahms's way is not only desirable but infinitely preferable. They distrust far-flung ambition and wild-eyed aspiration, for they know the destructive element in daemonism, and in such persons as Adolf Hitler they rightly see the ultimate eruption of decadent Romanticism. They go in fear of dangerous men and all those who would stand upon the mountain top shaking a fist at God. They may admire from a distance, but they do not seek involvement. They are also those who acquiesce in if they do not actually demand the 'toning down' of the great art works, which tend towards sedition as all true art does, reducing everything to the common cliché of 'great classics'. They have youths and the dreams of youth; but they tend to diminish the dream in the interests of what they believe to be 'maturing', and when they think they grow up and put foolish enthusiasms behind them, they in fact only grow old. Of them Brahms is perhaps the natural representative in music. He was much more than that, of course, for he was an artist of genius, and even prudent genius (if that paradox is not too great) is unencumbered with the surface prejudices and preconceptions of a social retrenchment. Yet Brahms perhaps represents the idealization of the bourgeois world of the nineteenth century as Mozart represented the idealization of the aristocratic world of the eighteenth. In most respects Brahms's music is at the opposite to Mozart's; yet it is so in the same way that the bourgeois romantic nineteenth century was the opposite of the classical aristocratic eighteenth century.

The Third symphony continues to illuminate in other directions also. As in musical logic and metaphysical content it is entirely characteristic of the mature Brahms, so in its thematic origins it represents him at his most typical. The second subject of the first movement is one of those lilting instrumental lyrics clearly derived from German folk-songs. The relationship between Brahms's themes and German folk-song has often been observed. He himself was perfectly aware of it. Whether it came directly from the folk-tune, as it obviously sometimes did, or whether the folk-tune set free the juices of his own melodic fertility hardly matters. What is beyond dispute is that folk-song lay at the bottom of it.

But it goes further than that. Lyric song was the fertilizing element in Brahms's musical creativity, especially his second subjects and slow movements, which too often for accident derive obviously from that source. No harm in that: folk-song is the root source of all music, and although art-song may not resemble folk-song, in fact at its most individual will not resemble it, and although symphonic and instrumental themes are seldom directly folk-song or folk-song derived, though they tended to be more so in the Romantic era, the soil is fertile and must at one level or another be cultivated at some time before an art-music truly nationally inflected can emerge.

German music has always drawn upon the rich treasury of German folk-song. Brahms may have drawn upon it more openly, more directly (some might say more honestly) than others; but the effect was much the same. Brahms was never a 'folk-song' composer in the sense that Vaughan Williams is called, not quite accurately, a folk-song composer, largely because there was a strong German and European tradition behind Brahms while there was virtually no English musical tradition, and if a revived English music was to be fertilized by the rich and hardly tapped storehouse of English folk-music it had to be done deliberately and in a sense self-consciously. It was inevitable too, in the circumstances, that the English 'folk' musicians should be set apart and labelled, for a new element was thus introduced, while in countries like Germany, Italy, France, Czechoslovakia (as it became) with a strong musical tradition the impact of folk-song on a musical style and idiom already formed was less prominent.

Yet Brahms's music is in many respects as much conditioned and influenced by the particular tone and inflection of German folk-song as Vaughan Williams's is by the English variety. Again because there was no English tradition, Vaughan Williams and his colleagues took some care to distinguish between thematic material based on folk-song and direct quotation of folk themes, but Brahms with the full weight of German musical tradition behind him felt no need to blush at a quotation or defend himself against a charge of misappropriation.

Often it is difficult to tell whether a Brahms melody is a folk-song or a tune based upon folk-song. In any case, his songs and lyric themes are so closely linked both to each other and to folk-song in one form or another that there is no point in trying to make pedantic distinctions. If the second subject of the first movement of the Second symphony is obviously a close relative of the famous song *Wiegenlied*, which is itself twin sister of the Waltz in A flat, Op. 39, and both are linked to folk-song; or the theme of the Adagio of the Violin concerto is an idyllic cousin to the sombre *Sapphische Ode*; it is nothing much to speak of but quite simply an integral part of Brahms's compositional procedure. Songs—his own as well as folk—are always cropping up in his movements, early or late. Pages might be filled with examples, and in the violin sonatas have been set down with diligence. For the purpose here, and since they seem not to have been noted so often, these two will suffice:

Example 5
(a) Wiegenlied

Symphony 2

(b) Sapphische Ode

Violin Concerto

If it is suggested that Brahms's reliance upon folk-song is evidence of some want of confidence in his own powers of creating melody, it may be in a small part true. But only a very small part: what is nearer the mark is that immersion in and use of folk-song and folk-derived themes was a Romantic propensity linked to the spirit of patriotic nationalism, itself also romantic in origin.

The second subject of the first movement of the F major symphony is by no means the only place where folk-song or the spirit of folk-song appears. The Andante is certainly based on one and the Allegretto hints at another. In keeping with its central place in Brahms's production, the F major symphony contains more folk-song references than the other three. The First and Second have strong internal links; but they are not, despite the *Wiegenlied* subject, predominantly folk links. They subsist rather in technical and stylistic features, like the high violin lines, the movement of bass figures, and the woodwind antiphonies. Much of this is repeated in the Third of course, for it is part of Brahms's hallmark —but in a different way, especially the high violin tessitura.

There is a fair case for arguing that symphonies 1 and 2 are complimentary sides of the same process in Brahms's creative orbit. The Third has a similar relationship to the Fourth, but from a totally different standpoint. Of all the symphonies, it is the Third which leans most heavily upon folk-based melody: the Fourth has small folk-song genesis, unless you call the bardic quality of the slow movement 'folk', but seems to review all the other aspects of Brahms's creative life ending with a decisive tribute to that older music, primarily of the North, in the magnificent concluding passacaglia. If the Third seems upon the surface an assertion of cautious optimism and the Fourth of confirmed pessimism, it is still only upon the surface. The *p* or *pp* ending of all four movements, the turning down of the hand at each final cadence, shows what the Fourth symphony finally and conclusively demonstrates—that Brahms spoke true in a larger sense than the particular when he called his Op. 117 piano pieces 'the cradle songs of my sadness'.

Where was the source of this sadness, the backcloth to this melancholy? A certain inborn bias of temperament, certainly; a certain bent of psychological introversion, confirmed and emphasized by his growing experience of life. His celibacy, often debated and dragged in as part of every possible kind of evidence for or against him, was a result rather than a cause of it. Why Brahms did not marry is a question that has often been asked, never satisfactorily answered. His own references to his bachelordom in later life veered between the portentous and the flippant. He once spoke with anger at 'those who turned me against marriage', referring obviously to the inmates of the Hamburg *Lokale*, who had cut a deep wound into his perceptions at a time when there was no Sigmund Freud to exorcize inhibiting ghosts; and by the time Freud was at work in Vienna, Brahms was too old and confirmed in his ways to worry about things of that kind. Those words he uttered to J. V. Widmann. His other excuse was that he could

not bear a wife's sympathy when things went wrong for him. We
have already turned that paltry idea into the street where it belongs.
Other references show that his opinion of women was low (though
his opinion of men was not much higher).

Or was it, quite simply, that he cherished a deep affection for
Clara Schumann whom no other could replace? It could be; and
if consummation with Clara was impossible because of the incest
substitute at work in one and possibly both, that would only make
the general drawing back more inevitable. At one time he thought
he was in love with Clara's daughter, Julie Schumann. It was
probably a kind of inverted sublimation of his deepaway love for
Clara herself; and it too must have foundered upon the rock of
incest substitute—with Clara, the mother-son rock, with Julie the
brother-sister one. Either way, the result was, and had to be, the
same.

Because of his high-pitched voice, his physical 'prettiness' in
extreme youth, and the shortness of stature which made him
awkward with women and girls, it was once on a time intimated
that homosexuality might lie at the root of his celibacy, and some
aspects of his music were pointed to in confirmation. So: Beethoven's celibacy was put down to syphilis, though no precise
contemporary evidence was produced. It is now demonstrated
that Beethoven's physical condition was due not to anything so
exotic as venereal disease but more mundanely and not at all
exotically to a rare but destructive form of allergy to his own body
and its functions. Brahms's case is simpler still, its origin not to be
traced to any fashionable bias towards the queer or the gay (or
whatever cant jargon may next year be in vogue), but to the plain
fact that he idealized and idolized one woman and in the face of
all others ducked the issue whether from attachment to her or
from natural circumspection and prudence, or both. In the end,
his private life follows the path and pattern of his music pretty
faithfully: after heady and toe-testing youth, a cautious but resolute approach and nothing taken for granted. He seems in fact to
have believed with the top layer of his mind that marriage was a
big gamble, and Johannes Brahms was not one for risking much
on a throw of the dice. He tossed it off by saying that when he

would have liked to marry he could not afford it but when he had money no girl would have him. A famous man no woman will have is a great rarity. It is unlikely that Johannes Brahms was one such. Another self-deception? Hardly. More likely just another aspect of the protective armour belt at work, deflecting unpleasant matter.

The probability is that far from maintaining an ideal and idealized celibacy, Brahms consoled his loneliness and satisfied his desire with the ladies of the Vienna brothels. A paradox maybe, remembering the youth's disgust at the sight and sound of the Hamburg *Lokale*. But no doubt the Vienna whores, at any rate those in Brahms's class of custom, were altogether more presentable and a generally superior species by comparison. Some of their names appear on his manuscripts, and no doubt some of those odd hesitancies, sudden outbursts, sharp clashes and blurtings that appear from time to time in his middle-years music originate in the confrontation of his demanding natural urges and impulses and the memories of his youth combined with sublimated passions in the context of the Schumann family.[1]

He was certainly not a misogynist, despite his poor view of the female sex. Goethe exorcised the ghosts of the women who haunted his memory by embalming them in books. Just how many ghosts are embalmed in Brahms's music is hard to say. Clara Schumann, of course; but that is hardly a case for embalming. Julie Schumann too; and others near or far. Agathe von Siebold is there, in the G major Sextet for sure; maybe elsewhere also, though again a ghost 'embalmed' is not quite accurate. But the idea probably is, for all that. Yet what really counts is the number of those women hidden away behind some unrevealed shroud of notes; concealed in some tender or aggressive phrase, testimony to Brahms's inner if by no means unconscious private life of the emotions and the affections. Hence too, no doubt, some of the depth of melancholy, the sadness sung from a lonely and unguarded heart pretending that it was guarded and quite content. There is in Brahms's music, as in Brahms's life, a half-concealed paradox centred upon the head and

[1] See Harding.

the heart's affections not in perpetual conflict or any naïve and commonplace fancy of that kind, but revolving in two confluent orbits which may touch many times but seldom quite succeed in interlocking.

With Brahms opposing principles tend to stand apart. Or rather, not so much to stand apart as to stand in a relationship to each other that suggests refraction more than direct interaction. His strong first subjects and lyrical second ones, often seen as representing the masculine and the feminine sides of his personality, tend to inhabit separate categories as well as separate melodic territories. If it is said, loosely, that the 'masculine' first subjects tend to be themes while the 'feminine' second subjects tend to be melodies, that does not carry us very far either, except perhaps to emphasize the division between the two. Yet although these principles and 'castings' are often separate and apart, Brahms's constructional skill seldom at his mature best allows the seams to show, the patchwork to replace a subtly woven texture.

Once again the Third symphony demonstrates exceptionally: the firmly plunging first subject and lyrical flowing second: the contrasting pull and thrust of the finale; the intervening middle movements biased towards lyricism and folk-song, but hinting beneath at the stronger emanations, the whole a resplendent example of both thinking and feeling in music, thought and feeling perfectly interlinked through true mastery of form. Brahms's themes frequently grow out of carefully planted and nurtured 'seed' or germ motives. Yet they never evolve with the organic inevitability of Beethoven, but proceed upon other and still original ways. The motto of the Third symphony is so deployed throughout the work that the whole represents a truly Brahmsian approach to cyclic form. The contrasts—harmonic, melodic, rhythmic, clashes of tonality, ambiguities of tonality, lead not in the Beethoven direction of final triumph, as in the Fifth symphony or ultimate consummation as in the Ninth, but to a particularly Brahmsian lack of positive conclusion rooted partly in his subjective consciousness and partly in the collective unconscious of the age, the breaking of ancient faith, the slow painful emergence of a new level of consciousness in the wake of the new evolutionary advance.

Brahms was neither a thruster forward of the evolutionary process, like Beethoven or as Wagner would be, nor an obstructor, a reactionary, like Hanslick, holding up pious hands or sitting Canute-like upon the shores of the oceanic advance of the modern world. He was a 'goer-with', and in that too he stands closer to the 'average man', the normal, intelligent, puzzled maybe, but in the end accepting, human being. *L'homme moyen sensuel*, perhaps; though in Brahms's case it must be added *l'homme moyen intellectuel* also. Again, a manner of speaking. Certainly the Third symphony brings the *sensuel* and the *intellectuel* into fruitfully close Brahmsian conjunction.

Yet there was little *moyen* about his intellectual capacity, whatever may be the truth about his sensual one. Brahms was Beethoven's near equal in intellectual force (though not in conceptual originality) and Wagner's superior, great though Wagner's capacity for sustained musical thinking unquestionably was (no one without massive brain power could have carried through Wagner's immense spans of music drama). After Bach he was one of music's supreme logicians. But he was also one of the most warmly romantic of lyricists. His lyric muse had not the light of the Romantic dawn upon it, none of the dew-bedecked freshness of the Schubertian flowering of song vocal and instrumental; none of Weber's related enchantments and magic of silvery glades and dark doomed forests inside and outside the human mind. The heart and mind into which Brahms saw and which he penetrated in his most characteristic music was romantic certainly, Romantic sometimes, poetically inclined, intelligently biased, though not of 'sense and sensibility' in the eighteenth-century precise sense. A bourgeois understanding and reflection again. And again it speaks most convincingly, the *sensuel-intellectual*, in the F major symphony.

This upon one plane. Upon another, closely related, the Violin concerto, the orchestral epitome of lyric Brahms. It was written for Joachim and crowned that friendship with a rare and noble beauty. The concerto came a year after the Second symphony, also in D, and like that powerful composition was made at Pörtschach-am-Wörthersee, the holiday resort in Carinthia where Brahms enjoyed a number of his best and most productive summer vacations.

Brahms's friend and lifelong correspondent, the eminent Swiss surgeon Theodor Billroth, wrote words about that landscape applicable to both D major works, upon hearing the Second symphony: 'How beautiful it must be on the Lake Worth.' The concerto went through more processes of change: Brahms altered it considerably from the original version shown to Joachim for advice (not taken) in the course of its putting together. 'Two middle' movements were rejected and replaced by the present Adagio, one of Brahms's loveliest creations, though he himself indulged in that rather childish form of word-play in correspondence, saying that the rejected movements were 'of course the best' and the substitute 'a poor adagio'.

Reading Brahms's letters and papers, and reports of his table or tavern talk, suggests that there was in him a vein of the childish and jejune, a lack of true seriousness, and that only in his music was he free of these minor imbecilities and bad jokes. Colin Wilson has called Brahms a case of arrested development, and he is not the only one to be so moved to speak; but I think it was not so much a case of arrested development of the innate and unique personality as a split between the real and the false in the character, which is the personality in action. There is the true and the false in every character—in Beethoven, in Bach, in Shakespeare, in Goethe, name whom you choose—but when the personality is properly integrated the true and the false cohabit, and so the true comes to direct grips with the false, and when all is functioning adequately expurgates it. But in Brahms one senses that certain areas are all falseness, concentrated knots of the non-genuine. Not large areas, only very small ones, probably not when added together more in totality than the falseness in most men of high gift and talent; but because they tend to be isolated and self-sufficient they come more openly to the surface.

Brahms suffered from inhibitions: all men suffer from inhibitions, but Brahms's lay nearer the surface and were more apparent and so contributed to certain inescapable false emphases. And much of this falseness is to be found in his letters and correspondence. Beethoven's letters are often jumbled messes of near incoherence or downright confusion; but Beethoven gives one the deep impression not that he is double or false dealing but simply that he is not master of words and so plunges often further into the mire, losing temper as well as sense on the way. Wagner was virtually a professional writer as well as a composer: Wagner's writings are often opaque but seldom either incoherent or naïve. But reading Brahms's letters one has only a small feeling that they come from the same hand as the music that bears his name. Indeed, the perky schoolboy prankiness and shallowness of many seem the direct opposite and perhaps complement the obvious seriousness, not always avoiding solemnity, of his music.

No childishness or solemnity in the Violin concerto though. The letter pertaining to it may irritate; but the work itself is as pure and *echt*-Brahms as the F major symphony, if for different though not opposing reasons. The slow movement, the 'poor' Adagio, fuses lyric song and extended form with immense subtlety; and the melodic line itself, corresponding as I have shown to the *Sapphische Ode*, each the reverse side of the other, derives both from folk- and from art-song. Confronted with Brahms's highly wrought melodic and harmonic structure, it is impossible to decide where folk-melody ends and art-melody begins, or *vice versa*.

The Hungarian finale also brings together several strands of the web of Brahms's creative texture. Nationally, it honours Joseph Joachim, the dear friend, and may tilt back to Reményi, he who set Brahms upon the road to international fame and onto the track of the Hungarian gipsy music also; maybe even a distant nod to the memory of Franz Liszt and the Weimar meeting which, however abortive it had in the end turned out, was a mark and milestone on the road of Brahms's arduous pilgrimage. And then, Hungarian and gipsy music was part of the Romantic addiction and cultivation. We know now, since Bartók, Kodály, Dohnányi, that the 'gipsy' music emulated by Liszt and the Romantics, including Brahms, was not the true, deep-down, root-in-soil Magyar folk-music but a superficial and unauthentic reflection of it; that in context does not matter, for the spirit that took the Romantics— and the romantics like Brahms—to Hungary and the gipsies may have come to it from the outside but was still honestly and in its way creatively motivated. For Brahms the gipsies were there all the time, first to last, D minor Piano concerto to Clarinet Quintet with many stops and diversions between. Joachim's Hungarian birth and ancestry merely brought it forth most strongly here in this most beautiful and most personal of Brahms's big orchestral compositions, a testament of friendship as well as of genius.

The Double Concerto, written nine years later (1887), and after the quarrel with Joachim over Joachim's divorce, in which Brahms took Mme Joachim's side and so broke the old easy intimacies, is some attempt at reconciliation, the violin representing Joachim directly, the violoncello probably representing Brahms obliquely, as some gruff, ready-drawn self-portrait. But old intimacies are never easy to recover and old friendships seldom revive in their entirety after serious rupture, and it is perhaps no great surprise that the Double is among the grittier and more stressful of Brahms's concertos. Though its lyric vein is, as ever, strong and purposeful, the driving force is somewhat strained, in basic conception rather than in execution, even a little analogous to that of the First symphony. Brahms once described the C minor symphony, before it appeared, as 'long and not particularly amiable', which was true of the parts rather than of the whole. The outer movements are long certainly, and if they seem more amiable now than they did to a generation bent upon setting Brahms up as the stern classical master, guardian of tradition, prefect of the Remove, they must still be taken as the serious emanations of a serious musical mind. Yet the two middle movements are both short and reasonably amiable. The Double inhabits a world half way in between: it is neither very long nor altogether amiable; yet it is from the true powerhouse of Brahms's genius, its concentrations and emotional as well as technical foreshortenings characteristic of Brahms's methods of composition at the height of his maturity.

What has this to do with freedom and the metaphysics of freedom? A good deal, since the growth and evolution of style is for the artist the outer symbol of the man's inward growth and evolution. Until well on into his thirties Brahms's music tended frequently towards Romantic expansiveness: the G minor and A minor Piano Quartets, the big Piano Quintet (which also had to struggle to find its right form, and eventually appeared as both quintet and two-piano sonata, another case of the abstract and the concrete pushing out of the same egg), and other compositions of some emotional as well as physical extension. 'Freedom is not licence' is an old and venerable cliché concocted to bar the way to adventure by the circumspect and the prudent, erected by the upholders of 'law and order' (a sure refuge for the incompetent) to guard against some reckless assumption of liberty or some aspiration towards godhead; and like so many clichés maybe it does contain a little grain of truth. But at the deeper, more potent and creative level it has no meaning but as another and more insidious form of 'freedom but . . .', and perhaps in the end licence is a necessary step along the path to freedom, as excess is to the palace of wisdom.

Brahms avoided, deliberately, both licence and excess. If he was ever tempted he soon put the temptation behind him. Also deliberately. And maybe that does set him in the league of 'freedom but . . .', and therefore of no freedom at all. Maybe. But it would be hard to say that in normal human terms Brahms shirked life and funked its ardours and difficulties. And not shirking or funking is inescapably involved with the acceptance of freedom. But that acceptance itself implies a triumph over death, a form of spiritual transcendence. Brahms all his life was obsessed with death and, though it may be too much to say that he went all his days in fear of death, he could never face the prospect of it with equanimity, still less with hope. The *German Requiem*, the Four Serious Songs: it is all the same in the end. Here is music of strength, of resolution, of stoical fortitude. But not of hope; not of the final vision. Not of victory. If he escaped the fatuity of 'freedom but . . .', it is because he did not deceive himself, did not deceive others. He did not shine false lights into the darkness, his own or the world's.

A melancholy man; a man of sadness therefore. Of a certain bitterness too, at the end. After the beginning and through the end. Also inevitably and therefore. He could not accept the ultimate tragedy of freedom, but he could and did accept the tragedy of consciousness. That sets him among men rather than among gods. But even that is not a simple, unequivocal statement or codification of merit. Men who stand upright sit higher than gods who do not.

Freedom can be accepted but abused. Only freedom accepted and realized stands upon the highest rung. And the air up there is too heady, too rare, too clear to support ordinary human life.

Beethoven found that out. Beethoven's last music is full of the sense of ultimate freedom, mystical penetration of the infinite; but it contains also moments of the most profound regret for all that human life means to normal human beings but which must be abandoned upon that mountain top. Beethoven said: 'Whoever understands my music will henceforth be free of the misery of the world.' But the road to that freedom entails also loss, loss of the human joys along with the human and sometimes inhuman pains, the untold miseries of the world. Brahms could never claim through his music to liberate us from those miseries. But he does help us to understand them, and so to sustain them, at many vital points by revealing them to us in himself. He is in the deepest, truest sense, one of us. We may wish to be one with Beethoven: in our lives, our work, our pleasures, or sorrows, we are one with Brahms. We too as men in the world are reluctant to take up the full burden of freedom, to accept the tragic consciousness. We may deceive ourselves that we do not have to; that we are free; that we are happy. Brahms at least gives the lie to that.

8 Sunset Glow

Though it followed but a bare two years after the Third, the Fourth symphony is so different in musical and emotional character that a full decade might have separated them. In fact they lie closer together than dates of first production suggest, for the keel of the Fourth appears to have been laid as soon as the Third had been launched, but the building took a while to complete. If the Third speaks of Brahms's clear-eyed, resolute, non-deluded metaphysics based upon the dual music-philosophical F-A-F/*frei aber froh* conjunction and juxtaposition, the Fourth turns powerfully towards elegiac tragedy, as though Brahms had suddenly seen the sunset reddening the far sky of his life, and perhaps not only of his own life but of the life of Germany as he knew it and the old Europe in general also. For in one sense the elegy of the Fourth symphony is a summing up of all that Brahms had worked for and achieved at the public level, all that he had given to and taken from the heart, mind and soil of Germany. Except folk-song, directly, though that too is there and honoured by implication. The first movement has its lyric flow over an exceptionally powerful and relevant intellectual structure. Hans Gal lights upon at least one leading principle of Brahms's music when he insists upon the melodic 'through line':

> Brahms, on the other hand, blended together his vocal and instrumental composition as naturally as Mozart or Schubert, for example; and a *cantabile* quality is the common denominator of his grand choral works and his symphonies.
>
> In view of the close-knit polyphonic texture of his symphonies, this may sound like a paradox; yet it is possible to sing every Brahms movement from beginning to end as though it were a single, uninterrupted melody. Through all its polyphonic intricacies the clear flow of invention remains distinctly recognizable as the mighty main stream of events. It certainly requires a great deal of concentration on the listener's part to grasp a whole movement as a single unit. By the same token, only a superlatively mature performance will escape the temptation of building up the whole from its component parts instead of letting every detail emerge from an intense perception of the main stream.[1]

Nowhere is this more true than in the Fourth symphony, which predictably receives fewer performances of superlative maturity than the other three. Of course, it is fundamentally true of all great symphonic compositions; of all compositions upon any extended scale at all that are not simply collections of incidence. But in Brahms it is true in a particular sense. It is also the reason why a good measure of tempo rubato is permissible, even necessary, in the performance of Brahms's music. The fashion today is against tempo rubato in general, especially in the 'classical' symphonies, and not least in Beethoven; but although fashion may decree otherwise, Brahms without some necessary element of rubato is Brahms robbed of an essential ingredient in his music. It is why some have charged him with drabness and even of 'muddy' orchestration.

The transition from the Third symphony to the Fourth, from

[1] pp. 212–13.

the metaphysical speculations upon *frei aber froh* to the stoic elegy
of the Fourth, will surprise no one who has attended to the down-
ward fall, the quietly resigned or softly conciliatory ending of all
four movements of the Third. The Fourth is indeed a vessel of
Brahms's profound sadness. I have called it elegiac tragedy, and
most commentators have seen it as essentially tragic; Tovey
referred to it as 'one of the rarest things in classical music, a
symphony which ends tragically'.[1] Yet I think the assumption from
appearances that this is indeed full-scale tragedy is unacceptable.
Lady Gregory said to W. B. Yeats that 'tragedy must be a joy to
the man who dies', and there is no joy in what Brahms set down.
It has dignity, strength, fortitude; but not joy. Its final resignation
is well prepared for, not only by the three preceding movements,
but no less by the totality of his life experience. There are no
rhetorical gestures in Brahms, no angered shaking of the fist at a
personalized Fate or God; only resolute acceptance of the necessities imposed by an inscrutable Providence.

Hemingway again, perhaps, in the different context of the nineteenth century against the twentieth. Hemingway's famous words
that a man 'should not place himself in a position to lose. He should
find things he cannot lose', could apply to Brahms—even perhaps
including the matter of marriage, the immediate text of the Hemingway conversation. Brahms tried to find things he could not
lose: it was part of the prudent caution with which he proceeded
through life. But no man in the end can find things he cannot lose.
If he thinks he can he deceives himself; and whatever else may be
true about Brahms, that he would not deceive himself is indisputable. This is the burden—part of it at least—of the elegiac
quality not only of the Fourth symphony, not only of these late
piano pieces he called 'the cradle songs of my sadness', but of a
large and continually growing facet of his entire life and creative
work.

The great concluding passacaglia, the magnificent apotheosis,
of the Fourth symphony gestated long in Brahms's mind and
originated in Bach's Cantata No. 150. But more than that, it is the

[1] *Essays in Musical Analysis*, vol. 1, p. 115.

high-water mark of Brahms's variation writing based upon the old
principles of the pre-classical era as the piano variations upon
themes by Handel and Paganini are rooted in classical procedure
informed by the older ways and making full use of the modern
keyboard techniques and resources. The symphonic passacaglia
combines in a new way the abstract and the concrete in Brahmsian
music; and it too has origins earlier in Brahms's own work as well
as in Bach's. The orchestral variations once taken to be upon a
theme by Haydn but now known as the 'St Antoni' Variations
have been judged, like other early Brahms orchestral music, as
studies for larger scale undertakings, leading ultimately to full-
blown symphony. And that work too ends with a passacaglia, or
variations over a ground-bass, leading there to a resplendent re-
statement of the main theme. But even that is not the beginning:
the Adagio of the Serenade, Op. 16, is still another form of passacaglia, in that case fused with sonata form, confidently so-called.
Thus at the outset of his orchestral composing, Brahms confirmed
the predilection announced in his early piano sonatas for composing in 'sonata form' with the strongest contrapuntal ingredients.
The three themes reveal an interesting contrast in Brahms's
approach to this species of composition, in three different contexts, with at least two of them deriving from Bach (the one from
Op. 16 from Bach's organ *passacaglia*):

Example 6
(a) Serenade

Bach theme

(b) St. Antoni Vars.

(c) Symphony 4

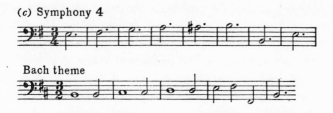

Bach theme

The chromatic character of the symphony theme is typical and extends its influence all through the succeeding thirty variations. Here is Brahms's fullest and most comprehensive testament of his skill in contrapuntal variation writing and of his immersion in a devotion to the music of the old masters of the pre-classical world.

Standing between the Third and Fourth symphonies, in form and content rather than chronology, is the B flat piano concerto. Again the musical logic is inexorable, the intellectual grasp of form immense. It has been held up as the *locus classicus* of the 'symphonic' concerto, in contrast to the exhibitionist type designed to gratify the ego of the world's peripatetic virtuosi—in the vein of the 'living reproach' again. It justifies that position when placed beside the showy bravura of the more empty display concerti; but as so often in the case of the honest Brahms, the old idea that it is a vast system of musical logic controlled by an intellect too formidable to allow of any passing indulgence of the senses or the pleasant fancy, is wide of the mark and does Brahms disservice. Indeed, there is much lyric music here, more various but a little less exalted than that in the Violin concerto. The four movements that the Violin concerto originally had appear here with the inclusion of a scherzo, itself thematically generated in the first scherzo of the Serenade in D, Op. 11. Gal's insistence on concentrating upon the 'main stream of events' and avoiding the temptation of building up the whole from its parts is particularly relevant in the B flat concerto, for in all concerti the danger of the soloist making play with fanciful detail is real, but if it is allowed to go on here the whole structure tends to come apart at the seams.

This, of course, is only in accordance with Brahms's most characteristic principles of composition, and nowhere, because of the medium, is it more clearly demonstrated. The horns sound from distant places, and we hear again the calls in the finale of the C minor symphony, the Andante and Adagio of the Horn Trio, many other works of Brahms's romantic vision (and of Schubert's and Schumann's as well, and also perhaps of Wagner's); and these strains might lead to compliant dreams of the lotus land. But Brahms very soon pulls the sound into the weight of the structure, so that the Romantic dream dissolves not into disillusion but into that force of mind and balanced foundation which are the mark and stamp of Brahms's best music. Thus the pattern is set; and it is followed through to the end—through the scherzo, with its mildly sardonic humour, through the Andante, with its flowing solo for the violoncello where even more both performers and listener have to keep the main stream firmly in view if elegant decoration is not to replace true musical substance, and through a finale as gracious as Brahms composed yet full too of that force and balance into which the concerto moved after its initial pages.

The B flat concerto is a product of Brahms's ripest and most consummate maturity. This 'teeny little piano concerto with a teeny little scherzo', as Brahms facetiously called it, tells us what a man without spiritual faith, without illusions, without inclination to excess or risk-taking, can make of life in its ripeness and plenitude in the self-adopted motto of *frei aber froh*, in its pleasure, its mild-eyed romance of middle age, in its tart testiness and hints of rough anger; in its strong determination and agreeable diversions. For all its poetic intent and content, it is *au fond* a work of musical prose and in honour of the prosaic life, though in no mean, snide or pejorative sense, but the simple literal one.

The deeper we go into Brahms's art, the more we find him the heir of Bach. This is not only because he was the greatest contrapuntalist of the nineteenth century; not only because the spirit of the old Germany as well as the new Germany was deep in him and his music; certainly not because of any religious faith or affiliation, of which Brahms had none but Bach a great deal; but quite simply because of the way in which Brahms completes a process begun by Bach who, standing as he did as one of the great pivot points of music, looking both forward and backwards, summed up what had gone before, anticipated what was to come, was a true prophet in the sense, defined by Walt Whitman, of revealing the indwelling source and principle of life. Brahms in his own way was also a revealer and prophet.

In the faith of Bach and the lack of faith in Brahms lie not only a spiritual division but a musical corollary. For Bach the Lutheran chorale was the foundation of his work; for Brahms German folk-song was the core and source of musical composition. Whereas Bach looked for the deepest musical secrets to the chorale, Brahms looked to folk-song, and the change summed up the progression from a sacred to a secular world- and life-view. But musically it was not so different after all, since both choral and folk-song are deep-rooted in, and the outcome of the life of, the people. One must therefore assume that both Bach and Brahms represent the innermost spirit of Germany across two formative centuries.

Around the age of fifty-seven—that would be about 1890—Brahms seems to have decided that the best of his life work was done and that he had earned a leisured old age free from the stresses of musical composition or execution. Like the English composer Arnold Bax, who in his late years would say that he had retired, 'like a grocer', Brahms intended to set the seal on his career with the String Quintet in G, Op. 111. He deceived himself, of course, for creative artists seldom 'retire' from working any more than they retire from eating and drinking. Exceptions come to mind—apparent exceptions anyway—like Rossini or Sibelius; but in general the artist spins art out of his heart and mind and bowels as a spider spins its web. Often the best work of all is done in old age, as with Verdi or Janáček.

With Brahms, though he did not live to a great age, whatever his conscious deliberation may have suggested to him, his creative faculty continued to bring forth music of the highest quality. The G major quintet, far from showing signs of finality, still less of tiredness, is one of the freshest and most 'Viennese' of all his works. It is pure Brahms, total Brahms, rejoicing in a plenitude of creative power and easy mastery: something of Schubert in spirit perhaps, but nothing of Beethoven, in a sense the bugbear as well as the god, the revered master. If Brahms intended it as his swan-song, he was obviously determined to bow himself out with grace and equanimity. The middle movements, it is true, invoke the sense of resignation and reflective melancholy that haunts so much of his most characteristic music. If Haydn could not prevent cheerfulness from breaking in when he praised God, Brahms could not prevent melancholy from rising somewhere, breaking in when he contemplated human life. It was endemic in his entire philosophical outlook. A wholly cheerful Brahms would be as unthinkable as a defeatist Beethoven or a neurotic Haydn.

That Brahms continued composition after the G major quintet may upon the surface be put down to his meeting with Richard Mühlfeld, the clarinettist of the orchestra at Meiningen where Brahms was a frequent and honoured guest and which was one of the principal German centres for the propagation of his music. Mühlfeld revealed to Brahms new possibilities in writing for the clarinet, and so inspired four contrasted works featuring that instrument—a trio, a quintet and two sonatas with piano. The trio—for clarinet, violoncello and piano—is often set down as among Brahms's lesser works; and so, in the context of his most commanding masterpieces, it may be. Yet it has much in it of the pure distillation of late Brahms, most notably in its spontaneous mastery of instrumental counterpoint and in the way the limpid tones of the clarinet so effortlessly reflect Brahms's autumnal mood. But most of all perhaps wherein the lightweight Andantino catches the 'sensibility' (*vide* Niemann) of those far-off days of nineteenth-century bourgeois life. Of course the clarinet quintet is the greater work, one of the loveliest and most imperishable of all Brahms's compositions. But something in the very lightness and insouciance of the trio endears it to all those who recognize the quiet sanity and gently sedative introspection (Neville Cardus's words) of Brahms. The trio indeed hints at more of the essential and comprehensive Brahms than may appear at a superficial hearing. It wears its contrapuntal learning easily, yet that virtuosity itself reminds us that Bach lay at the root of Brahms's art. The conversational element in the frequent dialogues between clarinet and cello reminds us of the homey, human, companionable Brahms beneath whose rough exterior and reserved manner beat a warm and often companionable heart. There is more than a hint too of the lilting Viennese music Brahms loved deeply, a kind of trans-mogrification of what went into the making of the *Liebeslieder Walzer* and the piano waltzes, his own version of those compositions of Johann Strauss which Brahms so loved and in which Felix Weingartner discerned 'something tragic'.

By the time the clarinet works were written, the old battles and disputations were left behind. Music was already moving into still newer phases in its evolution. Though Hanslick still lived and worked, and was still Brahms's friend and champion, and the echoes of battles long ago still exuded a rancid stench, the Brahms-Wagner quarrellings could only be kept going by diligent stoking. Wagner had been dead nearly a decade, his great work done, his battles won. Ironically too in Brahms's late works for the clarinet there is a kind of coming together, even a concealed sense of reconciliation, for Richard Mühlfeld had taken part in the first performances of *Parsifal* at Bayreuth, and so was intimately asso-ciated with the presentation of the last works of both Brahms and Wagner. Maybe it does not signify much in itself; but it does add a small honourable tailpiece to a sad and dishonourable story, the more dishonourable because the two major and central figures were hardly engaged in it at all.

But in fact the clarinet works were not Brahms's final composi-tions. Mühlfeld's inspiration may have set Brahms off upon a late burst of creative activity; but it did not end there. In one sense it only began there, with Mühlfeld and the trio and quintet (the two sonatas were not written until 1894). As important, and per-haps in the perspectives of history more important, are the sets of short piano pieces, Opp. 116–19, for it is in these that Brahms foreshadows many of the formal and thematic principles of the Second Viennese School of Schoenberg, Berg and Webern. The problem of continuous development in music appears to have occupied Brahms, whether consciously or unconsciously, in many of his mature compositions, as though he felt within him the need to break free from, at least to modify significantly, the rigidities of textbook sonata form. There are hints of it in many of his symphonic and chamber movements, as well as in some of his middle-period piano pieces. Now, in his last years, with the great bulk of his work behind him, he gave himself over to solitary communion with the creative spirit in solitary intimacy and alongside his sad communings with his own melancholy, and in so doing exposed a new manner of musical growth.

This new manner in respect of form may be seen as a corollary of Wagner's endless melody, though Wagner came to his idea first and pushed it further, much to the annoyance of Hanslick, who thought endless melody a 'logical monstrosity', largely because he knew nothing of the old music and could not understand that in the pre-classical, pre-sonata form periods melody had always been free and, within the modal context, endless. For Brahms, continuous growth had to come via form rather than melody; but it led along at least a parallel path. It was Ernest Newman who observed this process coming through in Brahms's late piano pieces, likening it to what Coleridge described in the plays of Shakespeare as growth upon the principle of a serpent making a fulcrum of its own body. Newman outlined his observations in two articles in the *Sunday Times* in July 1941, subsequently reprinted in book form in *More Essays from the World of Music*.[1] Thus Brahms, whom history has set down as the arch 'traditionalist' and implacable opponent of all that the 'New Music' stood for, shows that he knew as well as any the direction music would and must take, the way into the future pointed not by Liszt and Wagner or Brahms, but Liszt and Wagner and Brahms, each upon a ground of his own choosing, in the line of his own creative evolution, all three in the end the active agents of musical evolution, not just two of them against the third.

Schoenberg, whose extreme chromaticism, inherited from Wagner and pushed by him to such extremes that it led first to atonality and then to seriality by a process of inexorable logic, inevitable in its compulsive force, was also much influenced by Brahms. Schoenberg in fact wrote an essay on *Brahms the Progressive*, seeing in Brahms's best and most characteristic works the

[1] pp. 50–3.

creation of a musical 'prose' that has become an informing principle of modern music. Schoenberg was speaking mainly of Brahms's rhythmical patterns which, by altering the time values across the bar line without an indicated change of time signature, tended to break up the symmetrical patterns of rhythmical-metrical units of musical poetry.

Much of this Brahms derived from his studies in and understanding of old music, pre-classical music that is, for it rarely occurs in the 'classical' period. Although Haydn loved irregular phrase lengths he did not thereby alter the basic regularity of the rhythmical-metrical units or displace the regular effect of the bar-lines. With Brahms it is different, for he alters the rhythmic pattern by deliberate displacement of the bar-lines. This aspect of Brahms's music was particularly noted by Schoenberg when he began to undertake his wholesale reorganization of compositional technique.

But it is not only here, in his rhythmic patterns, that Brahms's influence bears upon twentieth-century music. There are at least two other points of direct relevance—his scoring and his evolutionary processes in his last piano pieces, especially where the thematic matter advances not by formal repetition but by one phrase growing naturally out of another, as (*vide* Coleridge on Shakespeare) B evolves out of A and C out of B.

Brahms has been accused of 'muddy' orchestration, but this will only appear so either to those who judge by incompetent performances or those who find all orchestration 'muddy' that does not fall in line with the romantically 'colourful' scoring of the Berlioz, Liszt, Wagner, Tchaikovsky, leading to the Mahler kind of orchestral deployment. And Brahms deliberately followed a different path from those masters, probably did not even read Berlioz's treatise on orchestration and certainly took no notice if he did. Brahms followed a different principle, and one that, oddly maybe, has been even more pertinent to the development of music in the twentieth century than that of the others. As Karl Geiringer put it, Brahms's scoring is 'fundamentally an intensification of the "openwork" [*durchbrochene Arbeit*] of the Viennese classical school. The motives and themes wander continually from one instrument to another, long-drawn-out melodies are divided among the various instruments, so that the lead is continually changing from one section of the orchestra to another.' [1]

And similar principles pertain no less to the layout of Brahms's chamber music, and even, 'translated', to his piano works. Brahms must have taken some of this from Beethoven's late string quartets, where the so-called 'sketch' treatment results in something analogous and itself arose out of the fundamentals, the abstract essence, of the Viennese classical manner in general. And as Gerald Abraham has said, relating the 'thickness' in orchestration of Schumann and Brahms and exposing their essential difference: 'Schumann's thickness is the result of incomplete grasp of orchestral balance and so on, lack of self-confidence leading to a continual playing for safety; Brahms's thickness is deliberate, part and parcel of his polyphonic musical thinking and the perfect counterpart of his emotional gravity.' [2]

It suited too, at its different time, Schoenberg's polyphonic thinking and emotional gravity. As Professor Abraham again argues, Brahms's orchestral style 'is in some respects an elaboration of a chamber style, a super-chamber medium called into existence for the expression of ideas too broad and powerful for actual chamber music'. And a chamber style in orchestral music, often specifically written for chamber orchestra, is another feature of the twentieth century, turning away from the grandiose and the flamboyant to the precise, the ascetic, the cautionary, emerging after the lush chromatic fulsomeness, reflected in the scoring, of Schoenberg's *Pelleas und Melisande*, the epitome and consummation of Wagnerian chromatic and emotional excess. Schoenberg's musical mind was in many ways very Brahmsian—Bach-Brahms-Schoenberg is by no means a nonsensical sequence. The constructive element in Schoenberg is reflected from Brahms; and the emotional gravity, though different, has a similar specific. And both were warmer, more emotional, less 'austere' than is suggested by trails they laid and which were too eagerly picked up by pro-

[1] *Brahms: His Life and Work.*
[2] *A Hundred Years of Music*, p. 162.

selytizing champions and adherents only too anxious to insist upon the unvarying 'seriousness' of their masters.

Schoenberg's theoretical seriousness and dedication came to dominate European music for over half a century; but it was Webern who exercised the potent later influence. Webern's immaculate precision on a very small scale itself derived from Schoenberg, the Schoenberg of the Three Little Orchestral Pieces (1910) and some of the short piano pieces. Webern also believed that once stated a theme has said all it has to say and must therefore be followed by something new. But if that is true, then the next step must logically be the end of thematic music and its substitution also by something new. This has in fact proved to be the direction post-Webern music has taken, with Gerhard, Boulez, Berio, many others. And much of it came through the last piano pieces of Brahms via the late works of Beethoven. Thus the musical 'revolution' of the twentieth century but demonstrates again the truth of Bartók's contention that in art there are basically no revolutions, only slow or fast developments.

At the end of his life Brahms knew Gustav Mahler but distrusted Mahler's music. The lines of work upon which he had with deliberation set out in the 1850s he adhered to with unshakable moral and aesthetic strength, not in a spirit of antagonism to all others but quite simply because he believed that was the way for him to go. If he did not trust the way music was going at the end of his life, that was partly because he discerned a want of seriousness as he understood it, though in fact it was more an inevitable change of direction as the nineteenth century moved to its close and the remorseless disintegration of European civilization rose to the surface. Oddly, had he lived to witness the rise of Schoenberg, though what Schoenberg stood for was certainly an aspect of disintegration, he would have found reason to regard the future with more equanimity. Schoenberg in fact links Mahler and Brahms: of Schoenberg's distinguished pupils, Alban Berg continues more in the Wagner-Mahler vein while Anton Webern distilled in his ultra-fastidious mind the lessons of late Beethoven and late Brahms. But the emotional impulse of Berg's music links Wagner and Mahler and Brahms in its lyric warmth, while much in all the Second Viennese School relates directly to Bach.

Thus Bach again stands as the pivot and creative centre of Austro-German music over those two centuries. Only the 'classical' era by-passed him, partly because his work was virtually unknown then, and partly because music had momentarily taken a tangential direction. For the classical Viennese period, far from being the central reality in European music was in fact an isolated phenomenon. A tremendous peak of achievement it certainly was: the central point of reference, no. Thus Brahms, the acclaimed traditionalist, looks both backwards and forwards, even as the great Sebastian Bach himself had. He throws a bridge across the Viennese classical period, to which he was aesthetically and stylistically pulled, though not exclusively as many for long thought, setting the polyphonic and contrapuntal principles and skills of Bach, and pre-Bach, into the loose context of sonata form, preparing in that as in several other ways the path for the Schoenberg-Berg-Webern emergence. He was, therefore, truly a traditionalist, in the largest, most liberating, sense, in no way as a narrow, obstructing reactionary. Those who have dubbed him 'traditionalist' speak truer than they often know: they think they mean that he upheld the old honoured ways against the iconoclastic new ideas; what they really mean is that he made the past potent and meaningful for the present and future, not as a museum to hide in but as a source to draw upon in creative vision.

Where then is the 'sunset glow'? Sunset is the end not the beginning; does not lead to new dawns, only into night. No doubt many would still say that the sunset glow of the nineteenth century and its romanticism, its sense of security, real or false, its belief not only in progress but also in its own superiority over all preceding ages, was indeed the harbinger of night, of the hideous nightmare as some would name it, of the modern world of the twentieth century. Those who believe that pull hard upon Brahms to find support for their view, for he represents for them a last refuge of sanity, integrity, sacred 'tradition' from a world which plunged headlong to its own destruction, morally, aesthetically, politically, militarily, all the rest. I hope I have argued sufficiently that Johannes Brahms in his life and work and person supports no such narrow and inhibiting outlook.

Yet that older world was ending, and perhaps Brahms knew it. If he distrusted the direction music appeared to be taking in his final years, he may have felt too, with that inner sense which makes all true artists the most sensitive register of their times, that more than music was coming apart at the seams. The sunset glow that is in his last compositions is perhaps not solely personal. Personal it assuredly was, for he held no firm faith in the afterlife, in some form of individual or spiritual immortality. He came to death not with joy, as Bach did, seeing it as the true goal of the human spirit, but with deeply rooted sadness and bitter regret. That faced with death there is only consolation for the still living is the burden of his view, propounded quite early in the *German Requiem* and confirmed beyond doubt in the Four Serious Songs of his last years, which have none of the hope and joyful acceptance of the New Testament but instead the disillusion of the books of Ecclesiastes and Ecclesiasticus from which he took his texts for the first three songs, with their sense of the inescapable brevity, even futility, of all human life. In going to St Paul's 'Though I speak with the tongues of men and of angels, and have not love, then I am become as sounding brass or a tinkling cymbal' for the fourth and last Song he seems to lift the veil of pessimism that haunts the first three and in fact haunted his own life. It may well be that the Songs are less a valedictory gesture to his own days which he knew must soon end than a reflection upon the end of his beloved Clara Schumann, who died in May 1896, and whose last illness filled him with dread and foreboding. If so, the turn to St Paul and the invocation of love takes on a direct reference. With Clara slipping away from him he had to console himself, and maybe that is why he referred to the Four Serious Songs as 'a birthday present to myself'.

Whether these great sombre songs were a valediction to Clara, to his own life which was so intimately linked with hers or were simply an old man's communings with death, they were also a kind of farewell to the great period of the German *Lied* of which he was one of the four undisputed masters. Though later composers, like Richard Strauss, wrote *Lieder*, the royal line virtually came to an end with Brahms as, again, did so much else, not only in music but in European civilization. The true German *Lied* was one of the imperishable creations of the Romantic nineteenth century. Song-writing was not confined to Germany, for it flourished elsewhere on a parallel course, in France and Russia notably.

But it is to Germany—or rather Austro-Germany—that it owed its fullest flowering. Mozart had written fine songs, and Beethoven, standing as he did upon the brink of the Romantic dawning, looked forward to the rise of the *Lied*, most particularly in his song cycle *An die ferne Geliebte*, but also in many single songs. But the great age of the German *Lied* opened with Schubert, then passed through Schumann to Brahms and Hugo Wolf, culminating with Brahms's Four Serious Songs and Wolf's *Michelangelo Lieder*. Three basic elements went into its making—the flowering of German lyric poetry, the combination of settings of it for voice with the piano style of Mozart and Beethoven, and the Romantic concern with folk-song and folk-poetry. Out of these elements grew a treasure-house of song unmatched since the fifteenth and sixteenth centuries.

All his life Brahms wrote songs. Indeed, nearly a full third of his total output of music is songs, mostly solo but offering a number of duets and quartets as well. Among his first published works are two sets of songs, and the Four Serious Songs was the last of his compositions to be issued during his lifetime. (They were not quite the last music he set down: that came in the Eleven Organ Preludes he completed at his favourite resort of Ischl in mid 1896, though some were probably written earlier.)

Brahms's songs represent a world within a world—or rather, a world within two worlds; that of his own work considered in its totality and of the larger context of the German *Lied* itself. And if, as is so, song was the mainspring of Brahms's melodic invention it is not surprising that in his songs is to be found the essence of much that informs his more ambitious works of orchestral and chamber music. Much of his piano music too. Brahms's songs are of many kinds, with the strophic song, derived from the folk-

style, prominent. They range from the simplest to the most complex, especially the most rhythmically complex; and in mood from
the most unassumingly immediate to the most deeply philosophical.
It has often been charged that Brahms, for all his high symphonic
ambitions, his sustained feats of intellectual building, was essentially a miniaturist; and if it is true, then what is most potent and
enduring in him may be found in his songs and the short piano
pieces of his middle and late years. But it is not true: 'little'
Brahms without 'big' Brahms does not in the end make sense, if
only because so many of the physically small works, which must
obviously include his songs, are so often informed by that intellectual force which not only led to but had to lead to his large-scale
compositions. He may on occasion have faltered with the larger
forms, may have padded out some movements with academic
matter, may even have constructed rather than truly created big
works, notably in the choral field; but his power of sustained
musical thinking over large spans was endemic and could not be
avoided or evaded, for it was not spurious ambition to impress that
caused him to address himself to major works but the inner necessity of his creative faculty. If the smaller in Brahms is often contained within the larger, the larger is also contained within the
smaller. It may not be true to say that inside Brahms's small-
scale works there is always a large-scale one trying to get out; but
given his particular mind and genius, the big ones had to come and
were as authentic as the others. Brahms was indisputably a composer with brains; and if you ask him to forgo the exercise of his
intellect you require him to put an essential part of himself into
limbo.

It is precisely the intellectual content of Brahms's songs that
distinguishes them most from those of his colleagues. Emotion and
lyric impulse he shared with them, though both were distinctly
his own; and in the setting of words he was sensitive but by no
means infallible. Hugo Wolf, certainly Brahms's superior in sensitivity to poetry, concentrated almost exclusively on song-writing
and achieved the kind of perfection beyond the scope of Brahms,
because for Wolf the fusion of music and poetry was absolute;
whereas for Brahms, where there was a contrary pull, as sometimes

there must be, it was always the musical value which had its way. Schumann's genius was essentially lyric and domestic, in piano music as well as song: he could seldom handle form with Brahms's natural ease and mastery, though by concentrated effort he sometimes succeeded in reaching potent formal conclusions, as in the D minor symphony and the Piano concerto. Schubert could spin music out of himself apparently inexhaustibly, and his songs came with the spontaneity of flowers blossoming in the sunshine, at times in the rain, and maybe even surprisingly in the snow. But Brahms's musical mind was always coming from underneath, so to say. His songs do not lack spontaneous impulse; but one is constantly aware of a profoundly philosophical mind bending a song to some purely musical end, his immense skill leading neither to contrivance nor to unexpected splashes of colour but to ends primarily determined by some musical solution.

When a composition was brought to Brahms for his judgment, it was his custom to lay his hand upon the page so that only the top and bottom lines could be seen. If these did not show independence and interesting movement, he would dismiss the piece: if they did, he would explore further. The contrapuntalist's mind at work, of course. And he applied the same disciplines to his own music.

The Four Serious Songs constitute the epitome of the German *Lied*; not its most charming or romantic aspects, but certainly in its most powerful manifestations. For Brahms, the consciousness of death was ever present. 'Man dies; nor is there hope in dust', is nearer to his agnostic view than any sense of redemption through the intervention of some divine mediator.

For Bach too there was bitterness in death, as there must be for all men not defeated or destroyed by the world, terror also to some extent or other however revealed or concealed, for death is something that all creatures fear. But for Bach death and the prospect of death was made joyous by Christ the Redeemer. For Brahms there was no such hope or even possibility. The *German Requiem* omits all references to or mention of Christ (all translations which include that name falsify the meaning [1]); and nowhere does

[1] *Mellers*. Part Three; p. 119; Latham, p. 163.

Brahms see death as anything but the cause for bitterness and anger. If the living can be consoled, well and good; if they cannot, it is all the same in the end. Either way, death is not the firm friend but the eternal enemy, the more resented because inescapable. In Brahms, a sequence of falling thirds invariably appears as a death motif, whether the reference is direct or instrumentally implied. Wilfrid Mellers points out that the third of the Four Serious Songs is based on the same descending third motif as the passacaglia finale of the Fourth symphony. Thus the immense elegy of the symphony is unmistakably linked to those final songs of the contemplation of death. Final? Maybe not, after all. That St Paul has the last word tilts the balance at the last moment, the ultimate moment of an earthly life all but run its course. A small thing; but it signifies. And as Mellers also observes, the resolving thirds and sixths of the third of the Four Serious Songs result in music almost as completely thematic as the last Bach Chorale Prelude, *Vor deinen Tron tret' ich allhier* (tune, 'Wenn wir in höchsten Nöten sein'). The linkage is long and indelible, the more so because the end is almost entirely contrary.

At the end of his life too Brahms published his major collection of settings of German folk-song, those songs and their verses which had been such an inspiriation to him throughout his patient years; and this collection, the 'Forty-nine Deutsche Volkslieder', ends with that same song the melody of which he had incorporated as the theme for the variations of his first piano sonata, in C major, Op. 1—*Verstohlen geht der Mond auf.* Brahms did not miss the cue: indeed, he almost certainly laid it deliberately. In a letter to Clara Schumann from Ischl dated August 1894, he wrote:

Has it ever occurred to you that the last of the songs comes in my Opus 1, and did anything strike you in this connection? It really ought to mean something. It ought to represent the snake which bites its own tail, that is to say, to express symbolically that the tale is told, the circle closed. But I know what good resolutions are, and I only think of them and don't say them aloud to myself. At present, now that my sixtieth year is passed, I should like to be as sensible as I was at twenty. At that time the publishers of Frankfurt tempted me in vain to have something printed. In vain did Kranz offer me all the money which I as a poor young man had such difficulty in earning. Why this was so, it is not so easy to explain. At sixty it is probably high time to stop, but again without any particular reason.[1]

The imagery of the snake again. But it does not even end there. Brahms had still not quite done with composition: the clarinet sonatas, the Serious Songs, the Eleven Organ Preludes—these latter above all. The snake bit its own tail more than once, more complexly than in the repetition of a little folk-song. The last word refers unmistakably to Bach, and via the Fourth symphony, to that old-world Germany the spirit of which has been preserved by Bach and had now been perpetuated into a new age and a new Germany by Brahms himself. Many strands coiled back upon themselves, making the story more complete, more detailed, more comprehensive and therefore more notable.

He ended then in reasonably good spirits and with a tempered resignation. Some have called him a Stoic; and I have used that term myself. Yet I feel it needs and must have clarification if it is not to remain simply one of those conveniences of language thrown out to shield the mind from the need for accurate definition or precise meaning.

What is a Stoic and what is stoicism? The general idea is that both terms refer to one who bears his troubles bravely, accepts what fate hands out to him with dignity and restraint and does not set great store upon human happiness. And broadly that is true enough, though vague and unscientific. Bertrand Russell states the Stoic ethic thus:

Certain things are vulgarly considered goods, but this is a mistake; what *is* good is a will directed towards securing these false goods for other people. This doctrine involves no logical contradiction, but it loses all plausibility if we genuinely believe that what are commonly considered goods are worthless, for in that case the virtuous will might just as well be directed to quite other ends.

[1] Litzmann, vol. II, p. 261.

There is, in fact, an element of sour grapes in Stoicism. We can't be happy, but we can be good; let us therefore pretend that, so long as we are good, it doesn't matter being unhappy. This doctrine is heroic, and, in a bad world, useful; but it is neither quite true nor, in a fundamental sense, quite sincere.[1]

In this light, Brahms as Stoic does not quite convince. Though he certainly tried to be 'good', as, musically, he understood it, I doubt if he did not care about happiness. He was certainly unhappy for most of his life, deep down and in the roots of himself; but he would have been happy if he could. Perhaps only his honesty prevented him from finding happiness, for he knew that for him to follow that road must be to deny something essential in his personality. He could deny either his integrity or his happiness. He chose to deny his happiness. But that seems at once to put him among the Stoics.

Epictetus spoke of happiness as 'freedom from passion and disturbance, the sense that your affairs are dependent on no one'. William Hazlitt, upon his deathbed, said: 'Well—I have had a happy life,' when to all outward appearances what makes for normal human happiness had quite remarkably evaded him. A dual side, then, to the Stoic spirit. And for Brahms—a half Stoic. He was not indifferent to happiness, even if he did not find it, either in normal or in Hazlittean terms, though the happiness which comes from good work well done was no doubt his, as it was certainly Hazlitt's. But the Stoic indifference, even at extreme hostility, to happiness was not a characteristic of Johannes Brahms. That suggests Hemingway again. In much of Hemingway one feels that to be happy would in some way be unmanly, a retreat from some fixed heroic image. In the later Hemingway this tends more and more to become an attitude, at its worst in *Across the River and Into the Trees*[2] and at its most affecting in parts of *Islands in the Stream*,[3] posthumously issued. In many ways this

[1] *A History of Western Philosophy*. Allen & Unwin, London, 1946. pp. 291–2.

[2] Cape, 1950.

[3] Collins, 1970.

turning from a genuine feeling to an attitude is an accurate reflection of the age in which it took place, when everywhere the attitude took over from the idea, when all became at the mercy of some passing fashion of the moment, some 'trend', without depth or substance. Brahms, though not of it, is a reproach to such a generation also.

But if his age destroyed Hemingway in the end, or he let it destroy him by destroying himself, his own did not defeat or destroy Brahms. Maybe some would call him the Seneca to Wagner's Nero; and though it does less than justice to Wagner, there is a shaft of truth in it. (It is also a simile rather than an historical equation, for in fact Nero was Seneca's pupil.) Indeed Brahmsian virtue and restraint, and Wagnerian excess, determined the character of the nineteenth century, the two in perpetual interaction. And furthermore that nineteenth century itself was a high peak of human evolution. After it the claim could be substantiated that though man's skill, and knowledge, expressed in his technology, has advanced unceasingly and in many ways spectacularly, his stature has not increased at all but has in certain major respects actually diminished. This is not a plea for a vague and spurious 'traditionalism', a laudation of the 'good old days', a gesture of impotence in a swiftly changing world. It is simply a charge that man has not responded to his evolutionary destiny, and that he has not used the real advances he has made to improve himself in any significant degree.

The men of the nineteenth century, at the poles of Wagner and Brahms, each answering in at least one important respect to the demands of evolution, were profoundly aware of the necessity for increasing and deepening the content of the human personality; of, that is, making a true gesture, not a merely rhetorical one, on the side of the angels. The nineteenth century failed; but at least it tried. Not since then has there been even a significant attempt to advance along some line of true and meaningful progress. In the end both Wagner and Brahms failed, with the century to which they belonged and of which they were two of the foremost representatives. What Thomas Mann said of Richard Wagner—that he was 'suffering and great as the nineteenth century of which he is the complete expression'—is true also of Brahms, if from a different standpoint. (In fact only Brahms and Wagner together sum up the complete force of the nineteenth century.) And if you listen to those deep, far-off soundings from ancient legend and myth which Brahms's music was always picking up, from the early piano Ballades to the slow movement of the Fourth symphony, you will know that he too, like Wagner, drew upon that deep deposit of saga in the German soul of which Thomas Mann again spoke.

Brahms is now nearer in spirit to our own times than Wagner. At one time Wagner was seen as the great modernist—and so in music he unquestionably was—and Brahms the conservative upholder of established tradition—and so in a sense he was also. But today we see the world through different eyes: sundry disasters, catastrophes and cataclysms have brought us down from the empyrean heights where Wagner and all the proud High Romantics would have man dwell in the richness of mind and spirit. The more homey Brahms, cautiously picking his way over difficult terrain, carefully examining what is presented to him and taking nothing for granted, misled and duped by no false optimism, impressed by no rhetorical bombast or vaulted magniloquence, is nearer to what we think and feel. If we have lost in the process, that is one thing: the fact of it is a fact of contemporary life. Even the young, noisy, often violent, in protest against all things past and most things present, are further from Wagner than they are from Brahms, for they will one day, when the spring tides ebb and the chill winds begin to blow, learn from Brahms and what Brahms was about, but they may never sail into the Wagnerian cauldron and tempest. Wagner's huge musical legacy is by no means a spent force; but through Schoenberg, Webern and one side of Sibelius (the side of strict economy and formal and thematic interlinking, observing Brahms's later piano works), and in the way he carried out if he did not initiate the process of 'linking back' to older music and composer, the influence of Brahms is perhaps greater if more insidious.

Today's composers do not recognize the influence of Wagner, and they do not recognize that of Brahms either, preferring either late Beethoven or some master from the far past in whose work they find inspiration and maybe liberation from the stresses and tensions and uncertainties of the present age, not as escapism but as starting point for the search for a fresh and refreshed vision. But when one hears their music, it is often possible to see not some direct 'influence' (in any case direct influences are invariably spurious and valueless, as the myriad mini-Wagners of a time ago effectively demonstrated, and a generation of mini-Parkers on the jazz alto saxophone have more recently shown), but an informing, underlying principle that emerges suddenly or is there all the time, even if they are not warm admirers of Brahms and proclaim, as Benjamin Britten has, not quite seriously, that all his music is bad. And even where he is 'bad' he is nearer to us than is Wagner, or some of the headier Romantics, for when Brahms fails he retreats to known ground, to the conventions of a codified 'sonata form' or maybe to some other device inscribed in textbooks for the confusion of students and the expulsion of creative originality. When our moderns fail they too may fall back upon the convention, the so-called 'rules' of seriality which can be taught as readily as those of sonata form and have just as dire a result upon the aspiring young or those no longer young who must seek a momentary refuge while the plugs are changed or the contact-breakers cleaned. But many in between, in the more recklessly 'romantic' years, relied only upon inspiration and when they failed fell over their own feet instead of those of some aged pedant or peruked pedagogue. One way and another, Brahms is musically relevant to us today, if in ways more subterranean than obvious, more devious than direct. That too is in character. In his character. He was never the pied piper.

He aged fast but died slowly. The end came on 3rd April 1897, from cancer of the liver. He suffered a little in the days beforehand, but not much at the time.

Three years and eight months later the nineteenth century he had so truly represented in one of its basic and essential aspects passed also into history. A further fourteen years and that European civilization which he prized and honoured plunged to its destruction, his own Germany, reckless and ill-directed, a mixture of hysteria and mounting lack of stability, ever since the 'dropping of the pilot', the dismissal of his greatly admired Bismarck, in the van, 1914 the death-knell of an age, a life, a world. And three years later still, 1917, the change became irrevocable: as historian A. J. P. Taylor put it—'In 1917 European history, in the old sense, came to an end. World history began.' [1] Not only Napoleon but Bismarck would have understood what was going on in Europe at the beginning of 1917. Brahms would have understood too, though it must have saddened him. Patriotically he would no doubt have cheered the German armies on. But he must have discerned that this was not localized conflict, not a repetition of the Franco-Prussian business of 1870, but something that would in the end destroy all he believed in, all he had worked for, not only the lights but the sun going out all over Europe. And so of course it was— and still is.

The death of that world is of importance in the present context because it was in a special and immediate sense Brahms's world, and so in that sense he is divided from us by more than a distance of historical time. That he has come through, has overcome that most difficult of barriers and can speak to our harassed times with a still firm insistence, a still resolute reproach for idleness, super-ficiality, frivolity, fickleness, all the rest, still gives us pleasure in the darkening hours and deepens our thought upon things of major concern to us; still warms the heart and refreshes the mind; bridges spans of music on our behalf from the bracing Handel and Paganini Variations to the lyric ease (but never flabbiness) of the G major sextet, the clarinet quintet, many of the songs, and face us directly with questions we have to answer, though we arrive at a different answer, in the *German Requiem* and the Four Serious Songs—all this and more is tribute to his achievement and to his genius. Say what you will, and much has been said, and probably will be said, but here is a man—and a composer. He cannot give us everything; he cannot give us all that Beethoven can, or perhaps Bach. But he can give us much for all that. If he is remote from

[1] *The First World War: An Illustrated History.* Hamish Hamilton, London, 1963. Penguin Books, 1966, p. 165.

us, as all artists are remote from us because we know so much more than they do—*vide* T. S. Eliot—he is still one of us. And if we know something essential about the nineteenth century, that tremendous age which spawned us all and out of which our modern age was born and had to be born in pain and violence and a huge letting of blood, he is half of the reason why we know and understand it.

Like all men, especially all artists, he is something of an enigma, difficult to get inside. But if we press him, the juices still run.

Appendix

'*Neue Bahnen*'[1]

Years have passed—almost as many as those I dedicated to the early editorship of this journal, namely ten—since I appeared on this scene so rich to me in memories. Often, despite pressing creative activity, I have felt tempted; many new and considerable talents have appeared, a fresh musical energy has appeared to thrust itself forward in the work of many gifted artists of the present time, even though their works are, for the most part, known only to a restricted circle. I have thought, watching the progress of these chosen ones with the greatest sympathy, that after such a beginning one must inevitably appear destined to give the highest and most enlightened expression to the ideals of our times, one who would not reveal his mastery by slow development but spring armed like Minerva from the head of Jupiter. And now he has come, a young blood whose cradle was watched over by the Graces and Heroes. His name is Johannes Brahms. He comes from

[1] See p. 56.

Hamburg, where he has worked in obscurity, trained in the most demanding laws of Art by an excellent and enthusiastic teacher, and was recently introduced to me by an honoured, well-known master. He bore all the outward signs that proclaim to us: 'Here is one of the elect.' Sitting at the piano, he at once revealed to us wondrous regions. We were drawn into circles of ever deeper enchantment. His playing, too, was full of genius, and transformed the piano into an orchestra of wailing and jubilant voices. There were sonatas, though more lightly disguised symphonies—songs, whose poetry one would understand without knowing the words, all pervaded by a deep song melody—single pianoforte pieces, partly daemonical, of the most graceful form—then sonatas for the violin and piano—quartets for strings—and every one so different from the rest that each seemed to flow from a separate source. And then it was as though he, like a torrential stream, united all into a waterfall, arching a peaceful rainbow over the rushing waves, met on the shore by butterflies' fluttering, and accompanied by the songs of nightingales.

If he will now lift his magic wand over the massed forces of chorus and orchestra, even more wonderful glimpses into the depths of the spirit world will emerge before us. May the highest genius strengthen him for this, of which there is every prospect, since another genius, that of modesty, is also his. His companions greet him on his first journey into the world where, perhaps, wounds may await him, but laurels and palms still more. We welcome him now as a strong champion.

There is in all periods a secret union of kindred spirits. Bind close the circle, ye who belong to it, that the truth of art may shine ever brighter, spreading joy and blessing throughout the world.

R. S.

(ROBERT SCHUMANN)

The Manifesto (1860)[1]

The undersigned have for long followed with regret the proceedings of a certain party whose organ is Brendel's *Zeitschrift für Musik*. The said *Zeitschrift* continually argues the theory that the most serious minded and talented musicians are in sympathy with the aims it represents, that they recognize in the compositions of the new school works of artistic value, and that the arguments for and against the Music of the Future, especially in North Germany, have been fought out and finally decided in its favour. The undersigned regard it as their duty to make a public protest against such a distortion of fact, and declare that, so far as they are concerned anyway, they do not acknowledge the principles advanced by Brendel's journal, and that they can only regret and condemn the productions of the leaders and followers of the so-called New-German school, which in part apply those principles in practice and in part require the promotion of new and unheard-of theories which are contrary to the very nature of music.

JOHANNES BRAHMS
JULIUS OTTO GRIMM
JOSEPH JOACHIM
BERNARD SCHOLZ

Reply to the Above

(*Appeared in* Zeitschrift für Musik, *4th May 1860. Authorship—C. F. Weitzmann.*)

DREAD MR EDITOR,

All is *out*!—I learn that a political coup has been carried *out*, the entire new world rooted *out* stump and branch, and Weimar and Leipzig, especially, struck *out* of the musical map of the world. To encompass this end, a broadly *out*reaching letter was thought *out* and sent *out* to the chosen-*out* faithful of all lands, in which boldly

[1] See pp. 110. ff.

out-spoken protest was made against the increasing epidemic of the Music of the Future. Among the select *out*-worthies (paragons) are to be reckoned several *out*-siders whose names, however, the modern historian of art has not been able to find *out*. Nevertheless, should the avalanche of signatures widen *out* sufficiently, the storm will break *out* suddenly. Although the utmost secrecy has been enjoined upon the chosen-*out* by the hatcher-*out* of this musico-tragic *out*-and-*outer*, I have succeeded in obtaining a sight of the original, and I am glad, dread Mr Editor, to be able to communicate to you, in what follows, the contents of this aptly conceived state paper—

I remain, yours most truly,

'CROSSING-SWEEPER'

'*Public Protest*'

The undersigned desire to play first fiddle for once, and therefore protest against everything that stands in the way of their coming aloft, including, especially, the increasing influence of the musical tendency described by Dr Brendel as the New-German school, and in short against the whole spirit of the new music. After the annihilation of these, to them highly unpleasant things, they offer to all who are of their own mind the immediate prospect of a brotherly association for the advancement of monotonous and tiresome music.

(Signed) J. FIDDLER, HANS NEWPATH, SLIPPERMANN.

PACKE. DICK TOM AND HARRY

'*Office of the Music of the Future.*'

Select Bibliography

Books Devoted to Brahms Himself

COLLES, H. C.

(1920). *Brahms*. London.
(1933). *The Chamber Music of Brahms.*
Oxford.

DEITERS, HERMANN

(1880). *Johannes Brahms*. 2 vols.
Germany. Trans. Rosa Newmarch.
1 vol. London, n.d.

DIETRICH, A., and
WIDMANN, J. V.

(1899). *Recollections of Johannes
Brahms*. Trans. Dora E. Hecht.
Seeley and Co., London.

EHRMANN, A. von

(1933). *Johannes Brahms: Thema-
tisches Verzeichnis*. Leipzig.
(1933). *Johannes Brahms: Weg, Werk
und Welt*. Leipzig.

* EVANS, EDWIN, Senior

(1912 on). *Historical, Descriptive and
Analytical Account of the Entire
Works of Johannes Brahms*. 4 vols.
W. Reeves, London.

Select Bibliography

FRIEDLAENDER, MAX   (1928). *Brahms's Lieder*. Trans. C. L. Leese. Oxford.

FULLER-MAITLAND, J. A.   (1911). *Johannes Brahms*. Methuen, London.

GAL, HANS   (1961). *Johannes Brahms: His Work and Personality*. Trans. Joseph Stein. Fischer Bücherei K.G., Frankfurt-am-Main, 1961. Alfred A. Knopf, New York, 1963. Weidenfeld and Nicolson, London, 1963.

* GEIRINGER, KARL   (1936). *Brahms: His Life and Work*. Trans. H. B. Werner and Berna Maill. Allen and Unwin, London.

HENSCHEL, GEORGE   (1907). *Personal Recollections of Johannes Brahms*. Boston.

KALBECK, MAX   (1904–14). *Johannes Brahms*. 4 vols. Berlin.

     (1909). *Johannes Brahms: The Herzogenberg Correspondence*. Trans. Hannah Bryant. John Murray, London.

LATHAM, PETER   (1948). *Brahms*. Dent 'Master Musicians', London.

LEE, E. MARKHAM   (1916). *Brahms: The Man and His Music*. Sampson Low, London.

* LITZMANN, BERTHOLD, Ed.   (1927). *Letters of Clara Schumann and Johannes Brahms, 1853–96*). 2 vols. Edward Arnold, London.

* MAY, FLORENCE   (1905). *The Life of Johannes Brahms*. 2 vols. W. Reeves, London. New ed., 1948.

MURDOCH, WILLIAM   (1933). *Brahms: With an Analytical Study of the Complete Pianoforte Works*. London.

* NIEMANN, WALTER   *Brahms*. Trans. Catherine Alison Phillips. Schuster and Loeffler, Berlin, 1920. Alfred A. Knopf, New York, 1929.

PULVER, JEFFREY   (1933). *Johannes Brahms*. London.
SCHAUFFLER, ROBERT H.   (1933). *The Unknown Brahms*. Doubleday, New York.
SPECHT, RICHARD   (1930). Trans. Eric Blom. Dent, London.
WIDMANN, J. V. *See* DIETRICH.

Books on Other Composers and on Music in General

ABRAHAM, GERALD   (1964). *A Hundred Years of Music*. Duckworth, London. Also Methuen, University Paperback.

BRION, MARCEL   (1956). *Schumann and the Romantic Age*. Trans. Geoffrey Sainsbury. Collins, London.

* CARDUS, NEVILLE   (1947). *Ten Composers*. Cape, London.

CHISSELL, JOAN   (1948). *Schumann*. Dent 'Master Musicians', London.

* ELGAR, EDWARD   (1968). *A Future for English Music*. Ed. Percy M. Young. Dennis Dobson, London.

* HANSLICK, EDUARD   *Music Criticisms, 1846–99*. Trans. and ed. Henry Pleasants. New York, 1950. Gollancz, London, 1950. Peregrine Books, 1963.

* HOWES, FRANK   (1948). *Man, Mind and Music*. Secker & Warburg, London.

* HUNEKER, JAMES   (1899). *Mezzotints in Modern Music*. Scribner, New York. W. Reeves, London, 1913.

JAMES, BURNETT   (1967). *An Adventure in Music*. John Baker, London.
(1960). *Beethoven and Human Destiny*. Phoenix House, London.

Select Bibliography

* MELLERS, WILFRID	(1962). *Man and His Music : The Story of Musical Experience in the West*. Parts 3 & 4. Barrie & Rockliff, London. Paperback, 1969. Barrie: The Cresset Press.
NEWMAN, ERNEST	(1956). *From the World of Music*. John Calder, London.
	(1958). * *More Essays from the World of Music*. Calder, London.
SCHUMANN, ROBERT	(1965). *The Musical World of Robert Schumann : A Selection from his Writings*. Trans., ed. and annotated, Henry Pleasants. Gollancz, London.
TOVEY, DONALD	(1935) on. *Essays in Musical Analysis*. O.U.P., London,
	(1949). *Essays and Lectures on Music*. O.U.P., London.
WEINGARTNER, FELIX	(1925). *Symphony Writers Since Beethoven*. Trans. Arthur Bles. W. Reeves, London.
WILSON, COLIN	(1965). *Brandy of the Damned*. John Baker, London.
WOOLDRIDGE, DAVID	(1970). *Conductor's World*. Barrie: The Cresset Press, London.
HARDING, BERTITA	(1962). *Concerto : The Story of Clara Schumann*. Harrap, London.

Letters from and to Joseph Joachim (1914). Sel. and trans. Nora Bickley. Macmillan, London.

Books marked * are quoted in text.

Index

Index